Poetry

Poetry
Recitations for the Tantric College

Lobsang Chukyi Gyeltsen,
His Holiness the First Panchen Lama

Translated by Geshe Michael Roach
Edited by John Stilwell

Diamond Cutter Press

Published in 2010 by
Diamond Cutter Press
55 Powderhorn Drive
Wayne, New Jersey 07470

Website: www.diamondcutterpress.com

Cover design by Clare Cerullo
Interior design by Jade Lee

Printed in the United States of America

Library of Congress Cataloging-in-Publication Data available upon request.

ISBN 978-0-9765469-2-4

Contents ࿊

About the Poems ?❧

This selection of poetry is from His Holiness the First Panchen Lama, Lobsang Chukyi Gyaltsen. The poems are meant to convey the First Panchen Lama's own inner progress in developing the steps of the path, and also to illustrate for us how he conducted his life and practice in the external world, as a real example for us to follow. In each case, these selections are chosen to relate in some way to a particular *lam-rim*, or step of the path, that we ourselves are working on.

All of the poems that follow are selected from *A Brief Biography of His Holiness the First Panchen Lama, Lobsang Chukyi Gyeltsen*, found at pp 488-560 in the classic work on the lives of the masters of the lam-rim lineage: *Biographies of the Lamas of the Teachings on the Steps of the Path to Enlightenment, (Byang-chub lam gyi rim-pa'i bla-ma brgyud-pa'i rnam-thar*, ACIP digital text S5985) written by Yongdzin Yeshe Gyeltsen, Tsechok Ling (1713-1793), Tutor to His Holiness the Eighth Dalai Lama.

Almost all the poems are translated here for the first time, and were found by Master Tsechok Ling among ancient papers of the First Panchen Lama at the Trashi Hlunpo Tantric College, which His Holiness himself founded. Master Tsechok Ling notes that much of the poetry found in the biography was never included into the First Panchen Lamas traditional collected works, but has rather been taken from a secret tradition of chanting his poems at the tantric college, where the poems were preserved separately as *Recitations for the Tantric College*.

In his brief biography, Master Tsechok Ling states that all of the different compositions included there were penned himself by Lobsang Chukyi Gyeltsen. The works have survived down to the present day—

and the fact that they were composed by Lobsang Chukyi Gyeltsen can be understood from the colophons attached at the end of each.

This book is in two sections. The first part contains selected poetry, without any commentary, so that the reader may experience the verses in the beauty of their uninterrupted flow. The second section contains excerpts from the *Brief Biography* describing the personal, political, or historical circumstances surrounding each composition; by reviewing the circumstances of His Holiness' life when he composed each poem, one may more fully understand the verses.

May you enjoy the instructive, mystical, holy verses collected and presented here as a source of inspiration to reach your ultimate goal—quickly, in this very life. As *The Prayer of Samantabhadra* states:

Suppose you took all the precious jewels
From every single planet, in every corner
Of the universe, and presented them
To all the victorious Buddhas.
Suppose you took all the highest happiness
Of both gods and men, and offered these
As well, for eons that were equal in number
To the atoms that composed these planets.

Still, any person who heard these lines
Of the Emperor of Dedication
And because of them felt some hope
To gain their highest enlightenment—
Anyone who only felt this faith
But a single time, no more—
Would collect thus infinitely greater
Merit of the highest kind.

About His Holiness
The First Panchen Lama ॐ

Lobsang Chukyi Gyeltsen, the First Panchen Lama, was an incredible being. From an early age he studied and practiced diligently, and readily succeeded in meeting holy beings face to face, as described in the first poem in our selection *The Lady Who Came to Me,* composed at the tender age of 14 years old.

He lived in a time of war and strife when people generally only lived to 50 years, yet he himself lived to be almost a hundred years old. Geshe Potowa's biography describes him with the lines: "In Tibet there is a certain monk whose life story is enough to express the life stories of thousands of normal monks." And "The fame [*drak*][1] of this holy being extends even to India."

And as Master Tsechok Ling states in the *Brief Biography*: "this one monk, in a certain number of years, would surpass thousands upon thousands of other monks—he would set his single-pointed attention fiercely upon attaining the state of omniscience, and in this extraordinary aspiration his single life would embody the efforts of thousands of other people's lives.

"He went forth and made extraordinary efforts first in a major period of his life devoted to studying and teaching the sacred books—to the skills of learning and thinking about them carefully. The number of people at his monastery of Wengun swelled, with a great gathering of monks and an influx of the faithful from the whole surrounding area. He taught them books on the steps of the path *(lam-rim)*; and works on how to develop the good heart *(lojong)*; the *Great Book of the Kadampas; The Mountain of Jewels, a Book of Metaphors;* the various instructions on vowed morality; and "dissection instructions" on the stages of creation and completion in the secret teachings of the *Frightener, Highest Bliss,* and others as well.

"In addition he gave teachings devoted to gaining a correct view of emptiness; and then initiations into the combined practice of the *Secret Collection, Highest Bliss,* and the *Frightener;* as well as empowerments for the *White Parasol* and other secret paths. He granted the rite of permission to practice the *Compendium of Nartang,* as well as that for a great many Dharma protectors. He taught then extensively on how to actually put all these instructions into deep personal practice.

"More especially, he repeatedly granted the empowerment and instructions on the levels of both creation and completion within the secret teachings of the traditional three—the *Secret Collection, Highest Bliss,* and the *Frightener*—to the communities of monks at the Great Three monasteries of Sera, Drepung, and Ganden; as well as to those of Trashi Hlunpo, Gyutu Tantric College, and Gyume Tantric College.

"He gave in addition meticulous explanations of the work on the steps of the path by the great Holder of the Diamond; along with similar explanations of the four combined commentaries [to the *Secret Collection*], and *A Lamp for the Five Steps.* He granted as well, over and over again, meticulous explanations upon *The Revelation of Every Secret,* a commentary upon the secret teachings of *Highest Bliss.* So too did he grant, time and again, teachings upon the steps of the path, and upon the stages of creation and completion, to a great many people who had made their spiritual practice the entire core of their life—all meant as instructions to be committed to memory.

"Most especially, he granted—again as instruction to be memorized—teachings upon the steps of the path (all the way up to the inseparable pair) from the oral lineage of the Precious Lord, Tsongkapa. These he gave to many great adepts of Trashi Hlunpo—to his leading spiritual sons; as well as to the assembled monks.

"He also compiled texts for the oral recitation of rituals in the same three secret practices: rituals for becoming the Angel; for bringing the Angel before us; for creating the sacred vase; and for granting the empowerment—all in keeping with the sacred tradition of the Lord, the omniscient Je Tsongkapa. These works are used among all those who uphold the tradition of this precious Lord.

"Looking at all this we can say that this Lord, this Lobsang Chukyi Gyeltsen, both upheld and furthered the excellent tradition of the precious Lord Tsongkapa in the fields of both the open and the secret teachings—without ever mixing them up with other teachings, without ever adulterating them in any way.

"One of the most amazing deeds that our Lord ever accomplished was to institute the observation of the Prayer Festival on the Holiday of Miracles—echoing thus one of the greatest deeds of Je Tsongkapa himself. Concerning the festival, the Lord himself expressed the thought that this was one of the most excellent accomplishments of his current life.[2] We gathered an infinite amount of merit into our own and others' mindstreams by observing this festival.[3]

"News came then that the Omniscient One, the Victorious Buddha, His Holiness the Dalai Lama Yunten Gyatso, would be undertaking a tour of their region of Tsang. And so he issued an order that the Dalai Lama be formally invited there to Trashi Hlunpo.

"In what the history books then call the Days of the Monkey—which is to say, in the fire sheep year, during the waxing of the moon in the sixth month—a great assembly came forth from the walls of the monastery, headed by the various masters and their disciples: over a hundred of them on horseback outfitted in regal finery, galloping out to welcome the Dalai Lama.

"The Father and his spiritual Son came then first face-to-face on the soil of Chushar. A great clamor burst forth from the sky, as if the gods were striking their mighty drums; and from the heavens as well, the divine beings let loose a gentle shower of fragrant flower petals. Everyone there saw these things with their own eyes.

"He began a second major period devoted to his own meditation practice. To this he dedicated the seasons of autumn and winter, going into isolation and avoiding any kind of business. During these times he shut himself up in retreat, throwing himself into isolation and working to reach a great many different Angels.

"Thirdly then came a major period of public work. Here he devoted the spring and later months of summer to touring the areas of Nyangu, Shap, Shang, Tun, and other such places. He accepted there requests to teach or advise, and did so in ways that were always based on the Dharma—working for example to fulfill the needs of a great number of local officials, as well as crowds of both monks and laypeople.

"In the late autumn (of 1622), a large military force of Mongolians suddenly arrived at Janggyab. At the order of the Regent, and various generals and ministers, the Lord had to go out to try to make a treaty with them. But even though he traveled as far into enemy territory as Rongpo Dam, he failed to accomplish his mission in the way he had hoped to.

"He stayed at Drepung Monastery then for some time, trying to accumulate the karma for protecting life by helping both Sera and Drepung monasteries, through the gifts of both the Dharma and material support. One thing especially he undertook. There was a silver-plated tomb in which the remains of the Omniscient One, Sunam Gyatso, were interred. (This was His Holiness the 3rd Dalai Lama, 1543-1588.)

"The ornamentation around the entrance to the tomb had all broken apart, and everything was in a state of disrepair. Thinking that it would set in motion auspicious forces, and also help keep the teachings healthy in the world, the Lord set about having the entire tomb renovated, using great quantities of precious material like gold and turquoise. He also ordered the preparation of exquisite, personal ritual instruments of the same material as the entrance way, for use by the Omniscient One when he had grown again to maturity.

"He moreover went to the places at both Sera and Drepung where there were statues of our Teacher, Lord Buddha, and presented each of them with necklaces of jewels and silken scarves. So too at each of the Great Three monasteries he repeatedly sponsored religious ceremonies attended by all the monks, making the traditional offerings of a meal and gift of money to each person. This karma completed, he went into a strict personal retreat at Drepung.

"The entire Tibetan army had been brought together at Kyangtang Gang. After eleven days of heated negotiations, the Mongolian cavalry suddenly made a lightening attack on the Tibetans. Reports that hundreds of people had died reached his ears. And so the Lord, with utter disregard for his own life and personal safety, broke his retreat immediately, making his way with haste as far as Denbak, in the company of several close attendants.

"The Tibetan forces were surrounded at Chakpori Hill, and the Mongol cavalry was about to make a second charge to finish them off. Gunfire and arrows were already flying like a shower of rain, and he simply stepped right into the middle of it.

"This divine Lord then approached the Mongol leaders himself and begged them to stop, telling them that he personally possessed a sizable amount of wealth and expensive objects that he would offer them if they desisted. The leaders agreed to follow the divine Lord's wishes, and the attack was called off right in the middle. The lives of nearly a hundred thousand soldiers were saved in this one heroic act.

"On this occasion, leaders from both the Tibetan and the Mongols came forth and made offerings to the Lord, to be presented in a religious celebration at Lhasa. They all agreed to put down in writing a list of their agreements; and then standing in the light radiating from the gilded roof of the Temple of Lord Atisha they took solemn oaths to stop their fighting, and observe a lasting peace.

"By bringing about this peace, a peace that was won by refusing to give the least thought even to his own life and safety, the Lord was able to prevent the destruction of both Sera and Drepung; in effect, he had saved the life of the very teachings of the Victor, Je Tsongkapa.

"Looking back on it in this light, generations of impartial sages for many years after the high and holy Lobsang Chukyi Gyeltsen—people who have themselves undertaken to continue this tradition of preserving the teachings of our gentle Protector, Lama Tsongkapa—have all declared in a single voice that the Lord was no less than the gentle Protector in the unequaled kindness he paid us, succeeding as he did in keeping the teachings of Je Tsongkapa alive here in our world.

"At that point though there did occur an extremely serious obstacle both to the teachings of the Victorious

Buddhas in general and to the spread, more particularly, of the teachings of our gentle Protector, Je Tsongkapa. It happened due to the shared karma of the people, and because of the influence of a number of powerful and evil demons. The Omniscient One, His Holiness Yunten Gyatso (the Fourth Dalai Lama), suddenly passed on to his paradise.

"There were great difficulties then in the ensuing task of recognizing the next incarnation of the Dalai Lama. Again, the revered one, Lobsang Chukyi Gyeltsen, gave his own personal material resources without the least hesitation. He took all the crude people here in our Land of Snows and bought their cooperation with gifts of money and things.

"He showed perfect impartiality to one and to all. Whenever it looked like some disturbance or military action might break out, he went to work using his compelling powers of love and compassion. He brought people to make their peace, free of any hostility for each other, and saved the lives of a great many evil people.

"He made special efforts to take the most violent people aside and give them a careful explanation of the laws of karma and its consequences, putting them thus into a peace-loving state of mind. Without any thought at all for his own needs, he brought a state of peace and tranquility to the entire populace of Tibet.

"He promoted a sense of spiritual cooperation among all the different groups of monks, preventing any outbreaks of discord. Most importantly, he found skillful ways to accomplish the unmistaken recognition of the supreme reincarnation of the Omniscient One, Yunten Gyatso. And again he put every effort possible into these labors, with complete disregard for his personal safety and even his life.

"In the end then, his efforts to conclude the process

of the recognition were successful. In the Year of the Great Drum—which is to say, in the male water dog year (1622)—the supreme reincarnation of the Omniscient One was conducted from Chonggye to Drepung Monastery. There the Lord performed the traditional ceremony of cutting the lock of hair, signifying that the boy had left the home life to enter the order. He then bestowed upon him the ordination name of Ngawang Lobsang Gyatso, (who was to become the "Great Fifth" Dalai Lama, eminent scholar and statesman)."

These are but a few examples of the greatness of The First Panchen Lama, his realizations, and mastery of the path. In general, His Holiness followed an annual rhythm of deep personal retreat; periods of personal study and teaching to his core group of disciples at Trashi Hlunpo Monastery; and then extensive lectures and tours among the general population as well as government and business leaders, to help bring the Dharma into every aspect of the daily lives of both the ordained and people with a normal family and career.

These aspects of His Holiness' spiritual life—the division of his time, taking personal responsibility, and his insistence that Dharma was meant to be part of the "real world" as well—are extremely important as a model for our own practice and work in the modern world. These are meant to inspire us in our own attempt to make the steps part of our own mind, by reading about the inner struggles and outer, worldly challenges which His Holiness himself faced in the same task.

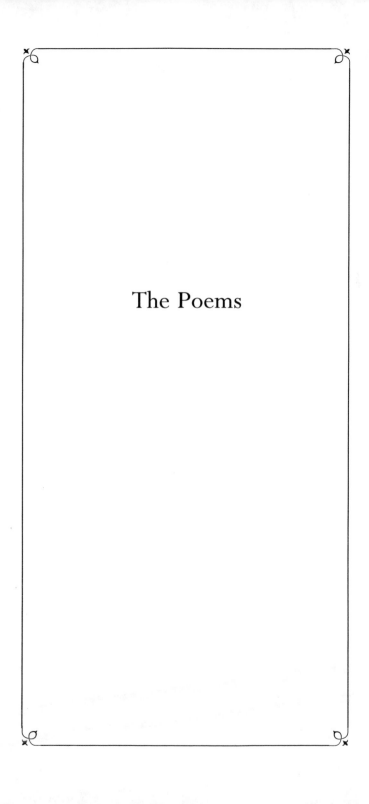

The Poems

The Lady Who Came to Me

Namo Sarasvateya.
I bow down to the Lady of Song.

This is *The Song of the Gods,* verses in praise of Sarasvati,
Lady of Song, Goddess of Words and Melody.

I bow first to the Conqueror, the Lord of the Spoken Word.

The Blue Lord melted,
and a wish-giving sea
surrounded me.
Crystal bubbles
struck from lines
of gentle sea-waves
smiled upon me.

I stood upon the shore
of liquid treasures,
sheltered in silken cloth
by the child of the lake.
The contours of her skin
shone as a babe's.

The meadow was green,
lapis stealing my heart,
gleaming jewels
spilled from the moon.

She was clear
as a flock of stars
upon the road
to deathlessness;
bathed in nectar
pressed from an emerald.

The feather-soft hand,
lovely, exquisite,
sipping the water

of Earth from the soles
of Her feet;
touched by the messenger
who cannot be seen,
but breezing soft.

The woman
wild in passion
gestured . . .
my mind
was torn to Her.
Lotuses spreading wide,
young and lovely.

She danced,
branches in a soft wind,
tendrils from the heart
of a flower.
The vault within,
where the falcon flew,
the inner bloom
was smeared with honey.

The young bee
forced the river
of the throat to rise.
The forest beckoned,
deep green, parrot's wing.

A glorious crystal palace,
fire of total bliss,
dancing window
to the salt
of a white lotus.

It lay atop the majesty,
shining in the nectar,

a thousand rays from each
of a hundred thousand
jewels in the sky.

Maiden mad in passion,
the atoms of her body each
a towering mountain.
Woman of wrath,
woman of beauty,
conch-shell ivy twining.

Glancing at me,
masses of deathless nectar,
splitting open
the lord of cooling light,
the knot of hair

the knot of hair,
lifted to the sky,
bearing flowers,
flower necklaces,
flower necklaces
soft wind of hair

all it a wing of white,
spreading over me,
arms of the divine,
You,
shining,
in your body
of the sky alone.

Face with two
beckoning me,
slanting lovely;
had it not been fingers
all together,
any one
would have done.

A shining leg,
thoughts unshaken,
a diamond opening;
when you're pierced
a thousand times,
what does
anything else mean?

Pleasure-garden lips,
smile of bliss,
a thrill up the spine,
from newborn crystal
dancing.

Pearl-white teeth peering,
soldiers in file;
sweet whispers,
flying to the caves,

masters who drink
the flower essence;
maidens
of the divine musicians
awake from their sleep
amidst the clouds,
and flee.

The womb of gold
stands abashed,
and turns to pretend
to meditate;
finger bracelets
of precious jewel,
exquisite,
embrace Her tight,

a pair of hands,
soft, tender,
sapphire lotuses
lift the secret lute

singing out,
sky's summer drum.

Lifting forth
that sweet burden,
breasts firm and flowering,
ripening maiden,
crowning jewel,

Deep contemplation
in bodily form,
what better spear
to shake my heart?

Saints
long since free
from longing
gaze on the wonder
of Your holy body,
shining,
and forget themselves.

Peaks piled
from softest bubbles,
dressed in strings
of pearls.

Her blouse,
dancing silk
of the gods,
soft, sheer,
enough to shame
the thousand feathers
of the Blue Lord.

She shines in ruby
lovely, true,
but the gossamer skirt
enfolding
emerges the victor.

The universe at play,
ten thousand
heart-stealing forms,
realm of the youth,
eight pairs full,
forever un-shifting.

Woman
of the Victors,
past present and future,
bliss itself;
I bow to you,
skulltrees planted
in the source.

I will think of you sometimes,
that shining light
of your sacred form,
and I pray
that by this simple thought,
a thousand rays of crystal light—
knowledge that sees
the entire galaxy of things
that can be known,
exactly as they are—
flies to every living being,
and rips from them
the darkness of ignorance.

And lastly now I beg
O Lady of Song your blessings:
Let the explanations I give
turn to jewels
that adorn the ears
of those with clear minds.
Let the debates I unleash
split open the brains
of those who dare
to speak wrong.

Let the books I write
become a necklace
that wise men wear
upon their throats. ♥

This has been written by myself, the monk
Lobsang Chukyi Gyeltsen, in my 14th year.

A Love-Poem to my Buddha Lama

Namo Guru Muni Indraya.
I bow down to my Teacher, Lord of the Able Ones.

I beg that you grant me
virtue and goodness,
Lama of the Gods,
Lord of the Able.
Let me rest my forehead awhile
upon those tiny rising moons,
the toenails of your feet,
a lovely string of priceless jewels,
a fitting crown for all of those
with delusions of worldly power.

Peeking over the summit
of the earthcore risen,
your holy body of gold,
is the magnificent orb
of your divine visage,
the daymaker;
and a smile that fills
the three realms of pain
with a thousand rays—
light, help and happiness.
Our faith lies in you,
Our Teacher.

You love those in misery,
those who have no protector,
with never a thought
for something in return,
or for some future karmic result.
'Til the day I reach
the inner heart of enlightenment,
I take my shelter
in the lotus below
the two holy feet
of the Conqueror.

Protect me, I beg you,
O Teacher of living beings,
and even the gods.
In billions of years of living here,
we were never able
even to hear the sound
of your sacred name.
And to hear it but once
removes all fear;
bestows the highest
of virtue and goodness.

I and the others here like me
are the crude and wild ones
who could not be civilized,
who shook off all attempts,
by other Victors
so full of greatest love.
We are the beings
of the days of darkness;
and we will never find
a protector or refuge
greater than you.

We wander around,
again and again,
in this cycle of life,
a place with no happiness,
a place that is filled
with thousands of miseries;
and we always wander alone,
there is no one that can stay with us.
Marriage of knowledge and love,
warrior who can do all things,
you know who I am,
you know my joy, you know my pain,
you know my good, my evil,
you know I've come to nothing.

You have rid yourself
of every fault;

you are a treasure
of every fine quality;
you never waver in spreading
help and happiness to others.
How could anyone ever think
of the way you've lived your lives,
and fail to feel faith for you
even inside their bones?

In your footsteps I left the home life,
but still I was never there in those days
to meet you face to face;
it's a sadness to me
that I try to stop
by making my mind a placid sea
where you can lay your reflection.
But still I cannot stop the sadness.
Let me bring you Teacher
once more to my mind.

Friend to whom all are beloved,
you without foes or family,
blazing sun of omniscience,
slipping down now, touching the tops
of the mountains to the west;
only a whisper left,
here in the final days.
I could hardly see
why I should live
the hours left to me.

But then you came,
and set my heart at ease,
showing yourself to me
here and now,
your holy body
mountain of virtuous deeds,
the smile upon your face;
the one who protects me,

the one who possesses
all eight highest powers,
a full moon set in the center
of the autumn sky,
winter on its heels.

I see the marks,
the wheel of a thousand spokes,
born from ten million deeds
of purest white;
and the webbing
between the toes
like that of a snow-white goose;
and nails of the toes
blazing in lovely jewel light.[4]
Let them touch me—
let golden fortune
touch the inner threads of my heart.

We don't live in times
when one can say with certainty
that the Highest of Teachers
walks here now upon our world.
But if we turn our minds
in a single point
upon this realm where
the mighty deeds of the Victors
engage in their cosmic play,
then perhaps you could deign
to make our dreams come true.

The powerful beings
of the other side
are about to attack me now—
I beg you, give me now
that right hand of yours,
shining like molten gold,
born of a thousand holy deeds;
reach it out with the grace
of an elephant's trunk,

and actually place it
upon my head.

It may happen that
I will fall again
into the miseries of the wheel,
forced by my past bad karma.
Even then may I always
remember you, Shakya Lord;
even then may the words
of the Able One's teachings
reach my ears;
even then may I never
lose this single thought,
this single sound.

You are the Supreme Teacher
of all beings, even of gods, and...

But where have you gone now?
Have you cast aside,
all of us, so pitiful, so lacking in goodness?
Are we left like children,
attacked by a thousand fears,
attacked by a thousand pains,
while our beloved father
sees how we suffer,
and then simply walks away?

The pain of it burns us,
the pain of being apart from you;
but then we know
that nothing can hinder
the knowledge and love and power
of the Able Ones;
and some little part
of the fire is cooled
by sacred water:
the truth of the words
you once left for us—

"I will always be the one friend
for those who have nothing."

I find some comfort too
simply in recalling,
simply in bringing to mind,
those beings who are the magical play
of our Savior's infinite wisdom:
the many Lamas who've taught me,
those who in person imparted to me
the excellent ways
of the Man of the Sugarcane.[5]

Imagine the amount of faith
and belief and perfect joy we feel
when we see or hear or think about
no more than the tiny slivers
of the holy deeds
of Shuddhodana's noble son[6]
which have come down to us
through other people.

How much more then
oh do I feel
to have seen you face to face.

Tormented by faith and devotion
triggered when a few faint scraps
of the One Gone to Bliss appear to me so,
the madman in a burst of vision
has woven this garland of delicate blooms.
Accept it, my Savior,
if only to take this pain away.

I must have captured
some small amount of good karma
from all of this,
a kumuda flower,
crystalline, white as a conch.
May the power of it

keep me under your care;
may I never leave you,
may I be born at your feet,
Lord of the Able,
wherever it is you've gone. ♥

The Death of a Disciple

Namo Guru Manjughoshaya.
I bow down to my Lama, Gentle Voice.

I ask you to come
and be in the center of the lotus of my heart,
Lord of Humankind,
who in truth is the wisdom of the Buddhas of all three times.
Wensapa,
keeper of a treasure house of the holy instruction
imparted
by the one who knows all, the King, Tsongkapa.

Fear—
fear for myself, approaching the age of fifty;
Years—
some 45 gone now, putting me among the old ones.
Distraction—
is the way I've lived, and squandered a human life;
What's left—
a butter lamp flame, once the butter's run out.

A brief life
here in the time of darkness, just a couple of days;
a waterfall
hurtling down the steepest rocky crag.
Lightning
in the sky—could you ever reach out and stop it?
Think a moment
about how life is; what use is there to love it?

My friends,
some high, some low, but almost all
gone now,
gobbled down by the heartless Butcher.
And now
here to his table come you and I, the very
next ones
for the King of Death, and no escape.

We must go now
down that narrow road of the state between,
far, alone,
and completely ignorant of the way.
Perhaps
it might be better if we put our things in order:
traveling companions
who will not deceive us, unending supplies, and no regrets.

Whatever
good things may come to us in this life now
end up
like a feast we enjoy in a dream, then wake.
Nothing more
than disgusting little seeds for the three mental poisons,
meaningless,
a way to while away the hours of our life.

Lots
of friends yes, dear to my heart:
chains
that drag me down to the three lower realms.
Sirens
lovely witches of the Isle of Singha;
Murdering
my chances for a higher birth, nirvana-butchers.
Go,
have a good time with the friends of your youth;
eat
rat poison because you thought it was a treat.
Go
sink in the hell-swamps of filth and rot;
stay there
for thousands of years—pain—pain—Oh pain.

Liquor
you drank, delectable, glass after glass;
all
it will bring you is mouthfuls of molten iron.

You will be
an ignorant beast in billions of lives
unable
to think a single clear thought.

You rush
here and there in your worldly work;
believe
it is something worth something, but it sends you to
pain.
A dream
you once had because of some random thoughts;
a life
of days and nights spent chasing a mirage.

The seeds
of the three poisons fill my mind;
I think
and I live in thoughtless sickness that's part of me now.
If I can't
cut it off in some desperate last attempt at a cure,
I don't
think I can try again; I doubt that now I can even live.

The very nature
of all things that are born is to pass away;
Here
in the darkest of days, life dies quick.
Now
I will stop spending my hours with useless things;
Now
I will take the essence from what I have left. ♥

Laughing in the Dark, a Song of Sadness

Namo Guru Manjughoshaya.
I bow down to my Lama, Gentle Voice.

O Lama who has paid me
the three kinds of kindness,
essence of the Buddhas
of the past and present and future;
I beg that you never leave me,
stay here seated on the top of my head,
spill down upon me a shower
of blessings and attainments.

None of these dear friends and
relatives of mine, so lovely to look upon,
are people I can trust to stay—
they play out their roles, come, then go.
Summer clouds that float together
then fly from each other at the whim of the wind,
impermanence itself, winter arriving.

Hundreds of days exhausted we worked
to arrange this party of worldly goods—
the thousand fragile petals of a lotus
stirred by the deathwind from the south.

Lovely luscious body of youth,
pleasure garden for children of lust,
exquisite golden vase, filled to the brim
with chewed-up food and piss and shit.

Ah the life of modern man
here in the modern world,
where proper order's no longer respected,
and the young die off before the old;
candles in a hurricane, we.

This city of illusion, three realms of suffering,
that can never bring happiness, that can only bring pain,
prison of terror with no escape,
a red-hot house made of iron.

We may be lords over every penny
and every scrap of food there is
in the thousand realms of a thousand worlds;
and then when we go we go alone
naked and empty-handed
standing alone and pitiful
in the middle of an entire desert
as our enemy comes to smash us down.

Driven by our negative thoughts
and by our past bad karma,
we spent our days here chasing
the objects of the senses,
in love with a pile of filth.
The story of our lives is the story
of butchers, wild dogs, and pigs.

The ones with brains, Buddhas and bodhisattvas,
these holy beings have gone on ahead.
And I'm left here the fool, all my own fault,
locked in this filthy body jail.

I pass alone, without a single companion,
over this sea of endless pain.
There is no shelter but you,
Lama and Three Jewels;
there is not a thing that can help
but you, the holy Dharma.

But these things I can never remember,
I casually live out the days of my life,
day after day, night after night
wasted without any meaning.
Perhaps I am stupid, or simply mad.

In the hour that The Lord of Death
comes to take you,
insane with fear and pain,
and the terrible visions
of the three lower realms
fill your heart and mind,
on that day finally
you will regret all this.

Try to see what's coming.
Come travel from day
to night to day
upon that excellent path
of taking care
how you act and speak and think.
Come I beg you
to the city of freedom. ♥

Begging the Buddha for Shelter

Guru Buddha Bodhisattvaya Nama.
I bow down to my Lamas, Buddhas, and Bodhisattvas.

I bow myself down
to the Lord of the Shakyas,
sending down a rain
of the holy Dharma
to clean away the stench
of three poisons
from all these people,
blanketed in the darkness
of illusion.

Lost in the sea
of the cycle of pain, fear,
shattered by waves
of karma and their own
negative thoughts,
ripped at by the sharks
of suffering,
people of misery—
protect them please.

People in the realms
of hell, starving spirits,
animals, tortured, burned,
no one to come to them—
but You do care;
protect them, I beg You.

Others here
supposedly gone
to the "higher" realms;
standing in a rain
of poison arrows,
the suffering
of all things that are born—

but You do care;
protect them, I beg You.

All who meet
are torn apart.
All we collect
is scattered.
All who are born
die.
All who rise
fall.
All these beings here,
tortured—
but You do care;
protect them, I beg You.

All these people
jammed between the fangs
of the demons
birth age sickness death
sink their teeth into them—
but You do care;
protect them, I beg You.

The times have changed;
people are completely ignorant
of the meaning of the teachings.
They don't need to rely
on the words of the Able Ones,
the ones who can see all things—

Instead they have new Master Teachers
who shows them directly
everything they need to know:
the unreal dream of good things
here in the life of pain;
the honey of food and money,
and behind it the honeybee's sting;
their entire life a waterfall

flying down from the mountain peak
of the truth that all things change.

Some run
like a deer pursued by the hunter.
Some take a stand
alone in a hopeless desert waste,
a visitor who just stopped by
for the enemy to slaughter.

Some seek pleasure
laughing they do wrong things;
then weeping
their face washed in tears
they come
to the karmic result.

The majority
of all these pitiful beings
are like spirits
in the state between death and rebirth,
harassed
by the demon of their own bad karma.
But You do care;
protect them, I beg You.

What greater shelter is there than you?
Take up then your sword, and in your compassion
stand for billions of years and defend
the rest of us, those beings of the days of darkness. ♥

A Song of Sadness at the State of My Mind

Namo Guru Manjughoshaya.
I bow down to my Lama, Gentle Voice.

I go for shelter, until the inner heart of enlightenment,
to the lotus feet of my holy Lama,
indivisible from our matchless Teacher,
King of the Shakya Clan,
a being who has freed himself from every fault,
and who possesses the highest of excellent qualities.

The wild river of mental afflictions
torrents of all the bad karma I've ever done
drives me helpless to the great ocean
of taking another suffering birth.
Pain, pain...think, think about it,
keep thinking how you go again
across that border, and then again.

Look at me, my companions in life—
look upon the terror of getting old:
ugly, decrepit body,
the ruddy complexion—gone
the power of muscle—gone
the dignity I carried—gone.
You can bring me a thousand delectables, yes
but I can't take them any more.
Memory—gone
the very ability to think—gone
one foot in the grave.

The forces within my own body
battle with each other,
not a day or night that goes by
without a thousand aches and pains.
I can't eat or do any of the things
I used to enjoy so much.

The doctors try to keep me together,
it's a losing battle. I know I will die now
and I regret my life.
Stricken by the sickness
which cannot be escaped
I cry afraid.

Look, look at the pain
of the world we live:
a lotus garden filled with wonder and happiness—
and then the mighty elephant of our own bad karma
tramples it underfoot.
Pain.. fire…cry out alone.

Think on it, think, those of you
who are wise—
we fancy ourselves rich
in our beloved circle of friends,
and a beautiful body,
and things to enjoy;
and then in an instant we're stripped naked
thrust empty-handed alone, alone,
into the next world.
It comes, comes now.

Watch yourself, if your are wise—
they will strike like lightning,
the five terrible signs
that your time has come.
No strength can stop them,
no army can stop them;
nothing you own
no secret mantra
no money
no beautiful girl
cheats death.

This then is written
by Lobsang Chukyi Gyeltsen,
in a moment of sadness

thinking about the fate
of the five kings who had their power [7]
over all the beautiful things
from the level called The Peak
to the lowest of the hells. ♥

While We Still Have Some Choices Left

I bow down to my lama, Gentle Voice.

From the depths
Of my soul I turn my heart
To the Lama
Of the Able Ones themselves:
To my Teacher,
The three high and precious Jewels,
Taking my shelter,
Then singing this song of my inner being
In words of reasoning,
From the path of the Word, open and secret.

The time
Is now, while we still have some choices left;
Don't
Leave fruitless, apples never picked.
Give life
Some meaning, devote yourself single-pointedly
To something pure,
That you can accomplish, and look back satisfied.

What I did
Up to now in my life is nothing hard to see,
But the journey
That comes after fills me with fear.
Better I think
Now to spend some time in preparing
For that
Long and dangerous road ahead:
Find
Someone to come along with me,
Pack
Some supplies that will never run out.

Back then
I spent my time enjoying life's tidbits;

Now
I look back, wonder what it meant.
Time
To stop deluding myself anymore,
And obtain
Some guarantees that I won't regret my life.

Since the day
I stepped into my mother's womb,
I have stood before
The enemy Lord Death, ripe to pluck.
He left
Not a moment left uncounted,
While demon liars
Whispered to me that I still had time.

A rainbow
Appeared in the winter sky,
Lovely
And gone in a single second.
This young
And healthy rosy body
Is a thing
That falls apart with each passing moment.

In the days
Of darkness, our lives are but a few hours;
A crimson flash
Of lightning from within some summer clouds.
The old
And the young die around us, out of order;
So now
Stop all this distraction, keep your eyes open—wide.

Family,
Friends and followers drift together;
Clouds
In the sky, then part and vanish.
Life
The bubble, cannot be trusted to stay.

Money,
Things, shining glories, nothing but a dream—
Come, quietly,
Set aside this farce of a life that lasts.

This body
Of a human being, possessed of resource and opportunity,
So difficult
To find, but so very easy to lose—
Only once
Do you find such a thing, and you have found it now.
Waste this chance,
Do nothing of meaning, and you're nothing but a madman.

Look
At all the objects there are, and all the minds that see them;
Just…there,
that is, if you never bother to look too close.
Delve
Into them, and they disappear in nothingness—
Throw
Your mind, naked as it is, into this empty realm.

Restrain
Your thoughts from chasing after likes and dislikes;
Come
Now to that precious treasure, the word of the Able Lords;
Live
In meditation upon the path of emptiness, with compassion at its core;
Never
Allow yourself to be separated from it, goodness for a lifetime.

As the years
Go by, you may not achieve deep analysis,
        based on learning and contemplation;
But remember, They have spoken that the mind is the root
        of the cycle, and leaving it too.
At least then
Try to work inside, bringing peace
        and self-control to your heart.

These words
Of advice capture the very essence
        of all the deepest Dharma.

Stay
Where your body is the Angel's
        the world and emptiness combined.
Stay
Where your only speech is to chant
        forever the song of emptiness.
Stay
Where your mind never stirs
        from the realm of the blissful void.
Model
Your life upon that of your spiritual
        father and mother: your Lama.

In talking
With you a bit about these things,
        I've done a great goodness.
By its power
May all the beings in the cycle of pain,
        in all three of the realms,
Stop all
The great cause, the source of pain,
        and everything it produces,
Thus gaining
With speed that highest state—
        the three holy bodies of Buddhahood. ♥

Admission into Agony

I bow down to my Lama, Gentle Voice.

Highest one, Lama, the one who is
Inseparable from the Lord of the Shakyas,
I beg You to come and seat yourself
Here upon the lotus within my heart.
Just bringing to mind what it looked like
When light shone from the jewels
Of the nails of your toes when I stooped to touch
them
Is enough to grant every wish and attainment.

From time with no beginning at all
Up to this very moment
I have drifted lost in this vast sea,
The cycle of pain, shattered by the waves
Of birth and aging and sickness and death,
Surrounded by sharks of countless pains.

The three lower realms have been
My permanent residence; most often
I burned in the flames of the lowest hell.
On rare occasions I managed to find
A body and mind in the higher realms—
But even then the eyes of my mind
Were clouded by layers of ignorance.

And so I passed those days enjoying myself,
Laughing the hours away with those who trained me
In the art of bad deeds, and friends
Who kept me company doing them,
Collecting the causes for my future pain,
And lost to that peculiar idea
That what is pain is pleasure.

And so now the fruit of my efforts
Has come to me, admission into the agony

Of this prison we live in, where pain
Rains down in never-ending showers.
A place where I can only sit and weep,
A place where no one can protect me,
A place where there can be no shelter,
A place where I can only wait and suffer,
Tears pouring down my face.

The red-hot sword descends on me—
And in this world how could it not?
Birth, aging, sickness and death.
Losing all that I love.
Gaining what I never wanted.
Working for things I never got,
And the pain built into my very being.

O they play here in this world—
Deluded by thoughts of grandeur,
Trumpeting for their arrogance,
The magnificent beings of pleasure—
The Lord, Pure One, Five-Arrow, the rest.
They take their pleasure for millions of years
Then take themselves to the inferno
Of the loest of hells, to burn, to blaze,
And smashed to dust by iron hammers.

O they fondled the breasts of celestial maidens,
Delighting in pleasure and play—
Then fell onto the sharp steel spikes
Of the mountain of shalma trees,
Impaled, split open in fountains of blood.

They greedily drank the nectar of the gods
In its thousand different delightful flavors,
But it turned to an ocean of piss and shit,
Rotting swamps of pus and blood.

O you who claimed to be the King—
Arrogant lord within whose power
Lay every pleasure of the entire globe;

But look at you now, down there on all fours,
An idiot beast with nothing to speak,
Forced to bear the burdens of men,
The helpless object of their exploitation.

Here I am, surrounded by family
And crowds of friends—I can hardly bear it
When they leave my side for even a moment.
But soon I will go to stand alone,
With no one to come along with me,
In that wilderness that we know nothing of.

O we may be lords of a land
That stretches from coast to coast,
With mountains of food and money
We've piled up by refusing to share.
But then before a few hours pass
We travel on with empty hands,
Leaving behind us even the body
That we thought was part of us.

We live without a happy moment,
Attacked by thousands of sufferings;
There is no good thing in these higher realms
That can grant us the slightest security—
Not our body or anything we own,
Nor family, friends, or followers.

Just stop and think for a single second
If you could ever bear the pain
Of falling back to the lower realms—
To the terrible body that your terrible deeds
Will force you to take: a being of hell,
A craving spirit, or an animal.

No I know I could not bear it—
But the turning of the seasons themselves
Will ripen the seeds of my own bad deeds
In luxurious crops of suffering.
I will writhe in pain that I cannot help,

And which even a purely enlightened being
Has no power to protect me from.

And so now, while we still have the power
To do something to help ourselves,
Let us try our hardest to follow the way
To the high state of the triple body,
Free of every one of the troubles
Which plague us in this life—
No more birth, no more aging,
No more sickness, and no more death. ♥

The Killer Child

Namo Guru Manjugoshaya
I bow down to my Lama, Gentle Voice.

Here first I pay my deepest honor
To the greatest spiritual sages of all:
To those who have entered the battle against
That foe so nearly invincible—
The three poisons of the mind—
And who emerged in the end victorious.
Bless me that, by these words I write,
Every person may be able to see,
To realize that the mental afflictions
And the misery that they bring to us
Are nothing less than the Lord of Death himself.

In their own right they are incredibly strong,
With the power that comes from constant habit
Over all the years of beginningless time.
And then the stormwind of looking at things
In the wrong way stirs them to further heights:
Towering waves of bad deeds I've done,
Of suffering and ill repute, ripping across
The hurtling torment of my own bad thoughts
A mighty and nearly unstoppable flow.

The Able Ones have reviled them,
And the assembly of realized beings
Has given them up completely.
The minute you indulge in one,
It drags you back downhill, by the very
Nature of things, without any effort at all.
Ah yes this stream of impure thoughts
Is strong and hard to stop.

Where on earth could you ever find
Anyone better than your own bad thoughts
At delivering misery straight to your door,

Weeping in the face of a thousand pains,
When the traitor with his cheerful smile
Has happily led you step by step
To what so soon will become a prison
From which there is no escape?

Think of the flames of the Hell of Fire,
And the Hell of Torment without Respite—
If they simply touched a single inch
Of the tallest mountain that exists in this world,
Even one made of solid diamond,
Then they'd turn it to dust in an instant.
Who but the negative thoughts within you
Could force you to enter this fire?

We stand on the desolate highland crag
Of an unbearable cycle of suffering,
Fear and terror where there is no beginning,
And neither any end...
Sadness simple without a shelter,
With no one to protect us.
And it was our very own negative thoughts
That dropped us here from each death before,
Not just this once alone.

Each time we indulge in one of those thoughts,
Each time we let the habit feed,
Then their grip on us tightens a little more,
And gradually tears us forever away
From ultimate freedom's shining glory.
And so here they stand, our mental afflictions,
An entire crowd of beloved friends
And family to the demons themselves;
How could anyone who sees how it works
Fail to see the ultimate foe?

These are the companions at our side
Who've invited home the incredible mass
Of all the bad karma we've ever done;
Theirs is the swift-flowing river current

That delivered us down to this shoreless sea
Of pain that perpetuates itself;
They are the massive open gates
To enter the realms of misery.
What better way then to spend our time
Than to seek out a thousand different methods
Of stopping them forever?

Think of a foe who comes to destroy
The body and life you have in this world—
Not just once, but a hundred times,
Or even then thousands of times;
How though could they compare in the least
With this enemy of our own bad thoughts?
Yet somehow still we indulge in them—
A mistake beyond all the other mistakes
We have ever made in our lives.

Come then, those of you with wisdom,
Who seek to drink of immortality,
The nectar of light forever free
From the chains of the problems of all three realms;
Come if you seek to flow instead
To the sea of bliss and happiness.
Come let us take our stand together
And make war upon the deadly trio
Of poisons that lie within our own minds.

Let us raise our diamond blades,
Tempered in a hundred thousand fires
Of faultless reasoning,
Burning swords possessed of the power
Of that one magnificent antidote;
Let us step forth and face the host
Of our enemies, all our negative thoughts,
So very difficult to conquer,
And let us strip their lives from them.
And when they sing those battle songs
Of the deeds of bloodied champions,
The wise will sing of us!

As for myself, I make here another prayer too.
Suppose it happens that every person
In this entire world—and I'm thinking here
Of the pleasure beings and the others too—
Suddenly rises against me as their enemy,
And tears away from me my very life,
Or all the things I need to live.
And suppose it continues on like that
From this very moment all the way
Through all the lives I have left to live.
Well I pray that even then I may never
Feel for them the slightest dislike,
Or any thoughts of anger at all.

And yet another prayer:
Suppose it happens that somehow one day
I find myself completely surrounded
By a mass of beautiful precious things—
Inner or outer objects of pleasure,
Thousands upon thousands of them;
Yet still may I see these too must pass,
These too are impure, these too an illusion.
May I never then even in my dream
Feel the slightest attachment to them.

And one final prayer as well:
May I learn to light the lamp of wisdom
Gained from the three-fold process of study,
Contemplation, and meditation;
May I raise this lamp in the endless dark
That hides from our sight the excellent paths
That lead to goodness of the world
And that beyond the world as well.
May I never again be wrapped within
This pitch-black misunderstanding. ♥

Ready to Die, or Live

Come Lord
You who have the three,[8]
My Lama, Keeper of the Diamond;
Come, sit
Here you the lotus
Within this one man's heart.
Lay
Your blessing there, so that I can rip from this space
My deadly foe,
My greatest fear, this compulsion for Eight Worldly Thoughts.

It's good
To live a long life—because then
You can practice
For year after year that excellent path
Of shining
White deeds, and then die happily:
Die,
With your mind crammed full of excellent karmic seeds.
A-la-la!
Because then its all the same, to live or to die!
So go ahead,
Do all the long—life prayers you like!

It's good
To have lots of money and things,
Because then
You can make more offerings, and do charity;
And then
Be quite as happy, when you're poor again,
Because then
You're freed from that special pain
Of refusing
To share what you have with others,
And the worry
That you'll one day lose what you have.
A-la-la!

Because then it's all the same if you're rich or poor!
So go ahead,
Do all the rituals for wealth that you want!

It's good
If everyone sings your praises
And your fame
Starts spreading to every corner;
That's nothing
To get yourself worried about.
It's fine too
If people criticize you—
Fame
Is only empty words,
An illusion
That cheats you in the end.
A-la-la!
Because then it's all the same, praise or criticism
So go ahead,
Make me as famous as you like!

It's good
Right now, if you're happy and healthy,
It's all
Just the kindness of the Triple Gem;
And you
Could just as well be miserable:
It's great
For increasing renunciation, and compassion, automatically!
A-la-la!
Because then it's all the same, happy or sad!
So go ahead,
Make me as happy as you like!

Don't you see?
It's all just the blessing of your lovely Lama:
To live, to die.
To be rich, to be poor.
To feel good, to feel bad.
When they sing your praises, or spit on you.

A-la-la!
Because whatever happens, just relax and let it!
So go ahead,
Have all the plans and worries you want!

These
Are the holy advices come down to us
From the glorious masters
Shantideva and Atisha,
And the Lord,
The Second Buddha himself.[9]
They turn
Deadly poison into the nectar of immortality.
A-la-la!
Because then you can turn a curse
Into a stroke of luck!
So go ahead,
Bring on all those dreadful omens you want. ♥

What Think You?

I bow down to my Lama

Father,
Holy Lama, I bow myself down at your feet,
Angel
As you are, the essence of all three Jewels.

Evil times,
These are, as the five degenerations spread.[10]
Hosts of demons,
Forces of the dark, grow ever more powerful.
Few can reach
The forces of light, the holy angels.
And the vast majority
Of humankind thirsts only for wrongness.

Most,
Even of the ordained, who have left the home life behind,
Are in their hearts
Corrupt, and deceitful—pretending to be something they are not.
And the teachings
Of the Lord, the Prince of Shuddhodana,[11]
Are fading,
Like a lamp when the oil runs dry.

And so
Those of you who seek for freedom
Should act now,
Try hard, take care, watch your mind.
If the very way of things
With causes is no more stable then a summer cloud,
Then the life
Of a human nowadays is a single flash of lightning.

Keep yourself now,
From being distracted by things of no real benefit;
The time has come
To accomplish your ultimate dreams—

No, not
That the time has come, but almost too late already.

This sea we live in,
The cycle of suffering, is bottomless;
And the pains
Of the lower realms especially unbearable.
If you have any brain at all,
It's time to turn and flee, as fast as you can.

If you piled up
All the meat and bone stripped away
From all the bodies
You've taken on and lost then over and over,
It would make
A stinking heap higher than the Himalayas.
And it's been spoken
That if you gathered together
All the molten steel
You've ever been forced to drink here,
And all
The blood and pus you've had to live on,
And all
The cool nectar of the gods you've ever sipped,
Then the great oceans
That cover this earth could never compare.

Even just the heads
You've had chopped off by enemies
As you struggled
And fought against each other
Would make a heap
Higher too than the highest of mountains.

The tears you've cried
As you sobbed in sadness
When you were torn
From beloved family and friends
Would equal a sea,
If they all flowed to a single place.

If you
Can be aware of the truth of these words,
And yet still
Sit there in comfort wasting your time,
Then I have to believe
That either you are mad, or your heart made of iron.

This lifelong companion of yours,
The things in life that seem nice to you,
Is about to desert you,
And he has called another to take his place.
Look, he comes, standing before you,
The Enemy, the Lord of Death himself.

That narrow path
Between death and birth is fraught with danger;
Who knows
Where our next life's destination lies?
And those who are wise
Realize that, if you really give it some thought,
It is nothing different
From the terrors of the fire of hell
Even if
We end up in one of the higher births.

If you have any heart at all,
Then look at yourself now, and let it break.
If you care about yourself at all,
Then make some kind of preparations for what is to come.
There is not a single pleasure
Here in the cycle of suffering
That you have not already tasted
Billions upon billions of times.

And yet what can you say
That you ever gained by enjoying them?
Think about it–
Did it all have any real meaning at all?
Give it some thought,
And from now on try to reduce your wants.

Come, offer your forehead
To your Lord, your Lama, Highest Guide and King;
Let it be a jewel
That they wear upon their feet, and never remove.
Throw your entire life
Into practicing that profound path
Which combines
Both method and wisdom;
The very cream
Churned from the infinite ocean
Of the Word of the Buddhas,
Both open and secret.

Wouldn't it be better if in this very life
You and I could attain the unending bliss
Of the three glorious bodies of an Angel?

What think you? ♥

One Day, in a Moment of Clarity

Namo Guru Manjughoshaya
I bow down to my Lama, Gentle Voice

I bow to the feet
Of the Lord, my Father, Mati Bhadra[12]—
That glorious body
Built of the highest bliss and wisdom
Of every single one
Of the Buddhas past, present, and future,
Masquerading
Here in this dance,
The outer form
Of a monk in the golden robes.

It happened one day
In a moment of mental clarity—
I was thinking a bit
On the essence of all the teachings I'd heard,
And the thought
Made me think of all the kindness
That my Lama
Had ever paid to me.

And then
I blurted out this Song of the Diamond,
Which is meant
To repay in some small way
My Lord,
My Lama, for all his kindness,
Taking everything
That I've gleaned from the years
Of scripture,
And whispered advice, and logic,
And expressing it all
In that extraordinary method
Where you take the goal
And use it as the path to the goal.

All because
Of the kindness of that one kind Savior,
I've been able
To attain this human form,
A body and mind
Complete in its resources, and opportunities.

So too, due to them,
I've been able to meet
In this life
With the word of the Lord, the Second Buddha; [13]
And been able to dress my mental stream
In the fine jewels of the three different sets of vows,
Learning to cherish and to protect
These vows and my pledges, the very foundation of
everything.

When I think of this,
I think of my holy Lama's kindness—
And oh how kind you have been to me,
My Lama and my Lord.

I've been able
To explore the meaning
Of the Word,
Both open and secret;
I know
How the cycle works,
This realm
Of causes and effects;

I have trained
In love, and in compassion,
And in the One Wish
For Buddhahood;
I grasp
The view of the world
Which grasps
That place beyond—

The way
In which all things are;

And I understand
The profound practice
Of the path
Of two secret stages.

When I think of this,
I think of my Lama's kindness—
And oh how kind you have been to me,
My Lama and my Lord.

I know
How to take the original state of things,
The three
Of impure birth and death and the state in-between,
And transform them
So they turn instead to the three holy bodies—
Becoming now
A power that ripens the seeds in my mind.

I know
How to look upon everything that ever appears to me
And see it
As the infinite dance of total purity.

I know
How to look down at my own body
And see it
As a divine form, indivisible empty clarity.

I know
How to listen to the world,
And hear every whisper
As the song of her secret mantra.

When I think of this,
I think of my Lama's kindness—

And oh how kind you have been to me,
My Lama and my Lord.

I have witnessed
The ways of the inner body of diamond;
I have seen
The doe-eyed girl with her three special virtues
Lying in the center
Of the child of the lake,
In the jewel
Surrounded by eight flower petals.

My mind
Never left that single point,
The magic play
Of my love for her;
The glory
Of her unfolded, wide,
Mother,
Daki of wisdom.

Up above,
The rays of a crystal moon
Burst forth,
And then again withdrew.

Later on
I went and captured
All the forest deer—
All the objects in the universe.

I used the snare
Of remembering what I had seen
Before,
When I was still in that deep meditation.
And then the snare itself
Turned into the body of an Angel,
A body made
Out of bliss and emptiness.

When I think of this,
I think of my Lama's kindness—
And oh how kind you have been to me,
My Lama and my Lord.

I coughed it up,
Using the drop of a lovely mantra,
At the center
Of the eight different spokes
Of the wheel of knives
Within my heart.

A masterful
Way of war it was,
To slash
In a single sweeping stroke
The throats
Of a thousand enemies,
The demons
That both the grasped and grasping
Were using
As horses to ride upon.

So too
In the center of the lotus
Of the chakra
Of every existing thing

I took up the lute
Made of clearest crystal,
Whose very nature
Was the diamond of shining wisdom.

I struck the strings,
Light beams of five different hues,
And played the song,
A melody of the three
Diamonds
That can never be destroyed.

With these glorious lines
Of the victory, in attaining
The glory
Of the true Angel's heaven,

I burst asunder
The knot of ignorance,
A bond
So nearly beyond all breaking.

When I think of this,
I think of my Lama's kindness—
And oh how kind you have been to me,
My Lama and my Lord.

And then there was
The highest channel of all,
Method
And wisdom melded together;

The very tip
Of the sprout of a child
Of the lake,
Finer than fine itself,

Was adorned
By a single drop,
The fruit
Of crimson and ivory elements.

And when
It was consumed,
Then ignorant
Disliking and liking as well,

Along with
That darkest ignorance
Which is their fruit,
Flowered and grew.

I died,
Without losing my life,
And once again
Sat and watched the struggle.

When I think of this,
I think of my Lama's kindness—
And oh how kind you have been to me,
My Lama and my Lord.

Then the sculptor arrived—
The mind, fast as thought itself.

It took up in its hands
The refined gold of the subtlest element of all,
And crafted the image,
An Angel's holy body, made of wisdom itself.

The body awoke
And did miracles beyond the mind to conceive.

I grabbed the universe,
All three realms, and devoured it in a single swallow.

At the very last
I murdered the host of Those Who Have Gone That Way,
And then had my way
With the holy Lord, the Woman of the Buddhas.

Aghast at what I had done,
I ran off into simple voidness.

When I think of this,
I think of my Lama's kindness—
And oh how kind you have been to me,
My Lama and my Lord.

And then from nowhere
Came again a rainbow across the sky;

The rainbow blazed
In the marks and signs of an enlightened being—

There was a virgin,
The cleft of method, the one of power,
And then came a boy,
Born of himself from the empty realm,
Drunk from the wine
Of the clear light of his home.

They united,
Never again to be apart:
Friends and companions,
Combined into a single thing.

They tore from the others
The immaculate, shining jewels
And a mass
of objects of enjoyment
Claiming them then
As their very own.

When I think of this,
I think of my Lama's kindness—
And oh how kind you have been to me,
My Lama and my Lord.

Now it may be
That none of these things actually happened,
But it is true
That through the kindness of my Lama
I've been able
To learn and contemplate that deepest Dharma,
And thus win this path,
Which is infinitely more rare
Even than the Lords,
The Enlightened Ones themselves.

And although this song
Is not something they'd ever have granted

To a man
The likes of myself,
Yet still it was sung
In secret, as you see it here,
By the Warriors
And their angel Women
Living
In the twenty-four sacred lands;

And within
This one simple song
Lies the very cream
Of the entire collection of tantras.

And so here it is,
Set down as a melody
By myself,
By Lobsang Chukyi Gyeltsen,
One day as I was recalling
The kindness of my Lord.

By the goodness
Of these few words I've spoken
May every
Living being that exists
Attain the holy
Body of diamond,
The shining glory
Of the two combined. ♥

Father and Son

Namo Guru Manjughoshaya.
I bow to my Lama, Gentle Voice.

You are the Lord,
A shining jewel among all who attend
Upon the Dharma Throne
Of the One Who Is Invincible.
You are The Savior
Of every single one of the infinite.
Gods
Possessed of that great good fortune.
At your feet,
Glorious One, Immaculate Empty Sky,
I beg you
To come seat yourself
Upon the filaments of the lotus
Within this one man's heart.

In the Paradise of Happiness
You sit before The Victor—
The Lord,
The One Who Looks with Eyes of Love,
Protector of the good,
And the greatest of all
The master sages
Who possess the five kinds of knowledge.
Look down on me with love, my Atisha.

You gained your enlightenment
Long ago, back millions of years beyond imagining;
And yet for the benefit
Of all us beings, who have no one else to protect us,
You assumed
The role of a human monk,
Keeping the code
Of the three different types of training.
Look down on us with love, my Atisha.

And the glorious one,
The Lord of Mystic Power—
Master Padma Sambhava,
Who succeeded in controlling
The evil spirits
And demons of Tibet,
Those beings
That defied all control before—
He was in truth
An emanation of yourself, Protector,
A piece cut off
From the magic of your wisdom.
Look down on us with love, my Atisha.

In these unbearable days,
As the five degenerations cover our country,
You have ventured forth
To the lands of the north,
Walking among us idiots
Wrapped in the darkness here;
And you shine forth
In a thousand rays of glorious light,
The help and happiness
That only the Dharma can bring.
You shine, Lighter of Lamps, my Atisha.[14]

You are the true image
Of all those who have Gone to Happiness;
Master of the secret world
Surrounded by the Buddha families.
You are the true source
Of the 84,000 heaps of Dharma,
And highest of guides
Amidst the community;
The assembled mass
Of every realized being there is.
Infallible shelter and savior, my Atisha.

If a person, o Father,
Kneels at your feet,

And makes gifts to you,
And with single-pointed
Thoughts of devotion
Begs you for your help,
Then you grant them
Each and every spiritual goal:
Both the highest attainments,
And those which are shared.
And you grant them with speed, my Atisha,

From this moment
Until the day that I reach
The heart of enlightenment
I know I need never
Leave, o Protector,
Your lotus feet
To go and seek
Any other shelter.
Come in mercy, take me with you, my Atisha.

Let me not
Take this foundation I've found,
This human form,
So hard to attain and easily lost,
And find out later
That I failed to do
Anything of meaning with it—
Luxurious crops of wheat
Left standing,
Rotting in the fields
Because no one went
To harvest them.
Bless me
To focus all my being
One-pointedly
Upon this single goal,
Getting some true essence
Out of this life.
Bless my mind now, my Perfect One.[15]

Let me rip
From its roots this savage demon
Out of my heart—
This enemy, the tendency
To see things as if
They existed from their own side.
Let me cherish
My family: every living creature
In every one
Of the six forms of life.
Let me devote myself
To the path where emptiness
And compassion
Are forever married.
Bless my mind to do all this, my Perfect One.

And I know
That whatever lies in the future,
In all my lives
That are yet to come—
Whether this poor beggar
Of a man ends up happy,
Or sad,
Whether good, or bad,
That it all
Depends upon you,
My one Angel,
Shining bright my Lord.
Never let me wander astray, my Atisha.

And when the seeming
Shining glories of this worldly life
Begin to fade
Into that final darkness,
May the glorious one,
Light his lamps,
Infinite forms
In infinite bodies of light,
Brilliant beams
That burst with his love,

Sent to me
For that final work.
Come in that moment
And take me, your worthless child,
To the Heaven of Happiness.

You made a pledge
That you can never change:
You said.
"I will be there, high above,
In the Heaven of Bliss,
The abode of the Thousand Gods,
I will be there
To greet you,
Any of you who are filled
With faith and devotion for me."
So come,
Let me see with my very own eyes
The truth of your very own words.

♥ ♥ ♥ ♥ ♥

Here next is the poem that he wrote to Dromtun Je:

Namo Guru Manjughoshaya.
I bow down to my Lama, Gentle Voice.

You are the god,
The protector of the Lord of Snows,
The one
Who Looks Upon Us with Love.
You are the heart-son
Of the glorious Lighter of the Lamps;
You are the Lord,
Whom they call the "Source of the Victors"—
But we know you best
Throughout this land
As Drom, the Victorious One.[16]

A son, a prince,
In truth the Lord
Of the tenth level itself,
Holding a white lotus in your hand;
But here, in order to guide
All us beings of impure minds,
You played the role
Of a simple layman with lifetime vows
And the pledge
Of lifetime celibacy.
In essence then
A true monk you were,
O Drom, the Victorious One.

It was you
Who received that highest form
Of prediction
Granted by the Victor Lords,
When they said
"There will come in the Northern Land
An upasika—
A layman with lifetime vows—
And he will be known
As 'the one who spreads the Dharma.'"
So here you are,
Protector of the snow-covered land of Tibet,
O Drom, the Victorious One.

All those
Who had ever Gone to Bliss
In paradises
Scattered throughout the universe
Took all
Of their compassionate wisdom
And combined it
Into a single form;
And this form too
They sent forth as you,
As the glorious
Founding father of the tradition
Of the Kadampas,

The Keepers of the Word;
As you who are our Father,
And the lord of All the Teachings;
As Drom, The Victorious One.

This life is fleeting,
Brief as a winter's day;
So the time has come
For me to devote myself
With a single mind
To the holy Dharma.
I can no longer
Allow myself to wander off,
Distracted by the enemy
Of all these eight worldly thoughts.
Bless my mind to do so, Dromtun you my Lord.

Let me throw off now
This burden of thinking
About what to eat,
And what to wear, and what to gossip about.
Let me cast aside
This life of attachment to this life.
Deliver me from this chronic disease
Of worrying only about myself.
Bless my mind to do so, Dromtun you my Lord.

Let me school myself
In love, and compassion,
And in the two
Different forms of the Wish;
Let me perceive,
Directly, that empty realm—
Free of all elaboration,
Free of anything being itself.
And let me travel
To the very end of the path:
The high secret practice
Of both secret stages.
Bless my mind to do so, Dromtun you my Lord. ♥

The Joy of Empty Sadness

Namo Guru Manjughoshaya.
I bow down to my Lama, Gentle Voice.

The never-ending flow
Of the empty realm of all things
Showed itself to me:
The stream of my own thoughts,
The revelation
That there is nothing that's real.
And then that thought
Melted into the diamond of the mind,
A single song
Of their indivisible union.

Look at all
My aging mothers—every living being,
Obsessed by their needs,
Their legs caught tight in the steel trap
Of living only
For the objects of their senses.
Look at them,
Locked in this prison with no escape,
Beaten, tormented
By savage feelings of pain.

The ruthless demon
Of believing that things could be themselves
Has invaded
The depths of their very hearts—
And so they cherish
Their own delusion, that a thing
Which never depended
Upon something else could ever be.
And so then they are
Attacked by a host
Of evil spirits,
Harmful ideas in which they see

This same thing
That is not a thing
And then for example believe—
Whether they know it or not—
That things
Must never change,
Or else
Have stopped altogether.

And so then
Their bodies are wracked
By every
Different kind of illness,
The disorders
Of heat or of cold—
Of liking
Or disliking things, ignorantly.
And then
They collect bad karma:
The poisons
Of diarrhea and vomit
Seep into
The veins, and the life
Of goodness
Is stolen away,
So that again
They assure that a mountain of suffering
Awaits them anew
In the cycle of pain.

At times I see
This way things appear,
And sudden tears
Pour down my face.
Sadness, pitiful,
Our fear and despair.
At times too I see
How things really are
And then all I can do
Is laugh out loud,

And a sense of peace
Spreads deep inside.

How do you feel,
My friends who know—
When you stand and look
At the people around us,
Tortured by happiness,
Tortured by pain,
All of it brought on
As these feelings of liking
Or disliking things
Infect their minds
Over things that are
Every bit as real
As the alluring smile
Of a young maiden born
From the womb of a woman
Who's been barren from birth.

Come,
Place all your hopes
In a Master
From an authentic lineage.
Devote yourself
To learning and contemplating
A wide variety
Of the classical texts
Which teach
The meaning that's literal.
Fill the very center
Of the fragrant bloom of your heart
With those ideas
Which are the deepest of all.
These are just a few little jewels,
Words that I've scattered along the way. ♥

The Peacemaker

Namo Guru Manjughoshaya.
I bow down to my Lama, Gentle Voice.

Please be my shelter,
Those of you who first undertook
To learn the problems and benefits
Of the cycle and all that's beyond it;
Who then spent every hour of their lives
Pretending to struggle to do what was right;
And then in the end had the realization
That the nature of the suffering side of things
And the nature of the enlightened side of things
Is but a single indivisible nature of things.

The great devil of thinking that things will last
Has invaded the hearts of all these people;
And so they spend all their time
Making their plans for the future,
Trying to eat the chaff in the air
And leaving the kernels on the ground,
Wasting their lives on nothing,
Ah the pain, the pain.

Oblivious to whatever bad things they're doing,
Or to pain or to the damage to their reputation,
They spend all their time refusing to share—
Piling up food and possessions, just for themselves;
And then without any power at all
To carry so much as an atom with them,
They pass to their death with empty hands.
Ah the pain, the pain.

After year upon year becoming accustomed
To the negative thoughts within their own minds,
They spend all their time wasting their time,
Addicted to frivolous preoccupations.

And then suddenly they find themselves
Locked in the prison of the realms of hell,
In fire and ice with no escape.
Ah the pain, the pain.

Amidst crowds of friends and relatives
They spend all their time strutting about
And then suddenly stands a single wretch
Alone in the midst of a wilderness,
Facing the ones who will cut them down.
Ah the pain, the pain.

They stand in the dazzling blush of youth,
They spend all their time deciding
Which lovely bauble they will wear today—
Will it be the gold, or perhaps the turquoise?
And then suddenly their naked bodies are thrown
Out onto the burial ground
Littered with the bones of those before.
Ah the pain, the pain.

With endearing companions, by the score
They spend all their time whiling away
The time in new and amusing pursuits;
And then suddenly the Lord of Death appears
And rips them helpless one from the other—
Ah the pain, the pain.

They build themselves a wonderful house,
As big as they can make it,
And spend all their time furnishing it
With the finest of chairs and soft silk beds.
And then suddenly there they lie,
Naked inside some niche in the ground,
On cold stone smeared with pus and blood.
Ah the pain, the pain.

They spend all their time obsessed with clothes,
A hundred cuts, all soft and fine,
And food and drink in a thousand flavors;

Then suddenly they are wrapped in a sheet
With that stale cake that they leave for the dead.
Ah the pain, the pain.

They spend all their time in arrogance,
Masters who control all the wealth
And power that lies in all three realms;
Then suddenly the terrible Prince of Butchers
Is dragging them powerless to his realm.
Ah the pain, the pain.

I know very well that my little song here
Won't set very well with the mass of people
Who spend all their time in chasing after
Things of this world to make them happy,
Trying to feel good, and not think too much—
Ah but then the pain, all the more pain for them.

So here it is, just a brief tune,
Ten times "Ah the pain, the pain"—
Scribbled down by that lazybones
Called Lobsang Chukyi Gyeltsen;
Sprawled out here on my bed after spending
All my time wandering these lands of ours. ♥

Parting Words on the Steps

Namo Guru Manjughoshaya.
I bow down to my Lama, Gentle Voice.

I can clear away this torment of life now
Simply by bringing to mind
My Heart Lama, full of kindness—
The one who has gone through this cosmic play
Over the last few millions of years,
Acting out the holy deeds
Of thousands of those who have Gone to Bliss
Here in the fortunate eon.

From this moment on, until the day
That I reach my enlightenment,
The question of whether I escape
The terrors of the three lower realms,
Or reach the higher ones, or even
Reach freedom from them altogether,
Is something which relies upon my supreme Lama—
The one who guides me upon this path.

But if now I go off to seek some shelter
That I imagine might be higher than my Teacher,
This one who's bestowed upon me all three
Of the different forms of kindness,
It would be like throwing away the highest
Wishing jewel for a trinket of glass.

This body and mind of a human we have,
So hard to find and with such great potential,
Are more precious than a worldly god's whole life.
Suppose that we grasp this fact, but even then
We waste the time of our life on this life,
And never fulfill its fullest purpose.

We'd be then even a greater fool
Than a beggar who through some stroke of luck

Is able to reach the Land of Jewels
But returns home naked and empty-handed.

Even in our everyday life,
The stupidest sort of worldly person
Would be every hour upon his guard
If he knew that his greatest enemy
Would arrive at his house within a month,
Or a year, but on some unspecified date.

Our one great foe though, the Lord of Death,
Is the same: we know he will come for us;
It's just that we have no certainty
About when he will make his appearance.
Alas then, we are more stupid than fools
To relax here without watching out for him.

This monstrous king of the realms of death
Eats away at our life from day to day,
And you and I have no guarantee
That he won't strike suddenly, even today.
How then can it be that we feel
Even a moment of mental peace?

Quickly now comes that final illness,
The incurable one, the unbearable one.
We roll in agony on the bed,
Covered in our own shit and piss;
The warmth of life begins to fade,
The breath comes hard and chokes the throat.

Relatives and friends stand weeping around the bed;
You're beyond the point of treatments and medicine.
You flail your arms and legs, you stare
With eyes of terror, because you know.
But still you hope then, don't you,
That some miracle will come and save you—
For you have spent a lifetime within
The illusion that somehow things will last.
But the Death Lord has already come

And mounted himself up on your back;
Lie there naked, lie there in shame,
Like there with hope, I can only laugh.

The time is upon us now,
And we must pass
Stripped of clothes, stripped of friends,
Stripped of even the flesh and bone
That we have loved so dearly,
Gone now to that empty desert
Where the enemy awaits
To strike his final blow.

Oh perhaps you were a powerful man,
A lord of the riches of all three realms.
But your power on that day ends, and you cannot
Take along with you even a single atom
Of all of the things that you used to own.
Surrounded you may be then by family
And dearest friends, but in that moment
Not a single one can come with you.

If in that hour you leave behind
Even the name you used to be called,
Then what need mention everything else?
Oh here we are, me and the others of you
Who perhaps are the same as me myself,
Ignoring this one great terror to come,
Completely engrossed in this life's affairs,
Which having nothing to do with anything.
Come please look after us, I pray,
My Lama, look on us with love;
We are every suffering person there is,
And we have no one else to help us. ♥

The History of Pain

Imagine single days and nights
Each one the length and breadth
Of all the history of pain
In the universe up to now.
Imagine then years made themselves
Of days and nights as long as these;
And now imagine eons too,
Made of years like those.
Imagine last a mass of these eons
Equal in number to the very drops
Of water in the ocean itself.

Suppose that it takes this long
To reach a single moment
Of the Wish for highest Buddhahood;
Or to accumulate any one of the deeds
We need to reach this state.
Still you must use your compassion:
Use it to stop any hesitation,
Stop any trace of feeling discouraged.
Reach your enlightenment.

You will be in pain here;
Never think of your own pain.
Don the diamond armor,
Endless diamond armor.
If you are a warrior,
A warrior of compassion,
Learn to live with pain.
I tell you now,
Learn this one thing first. ♥

Throw Off the Iron Fetters

Namo Guru ratna trayaya.
I bow down to my Master, the Three Jewels themselves.

I beseech you, my holy Lama—
You who are indivisible
From those who can never
Lead us wrong, the Jewels—
To come and seat yourself
Upon the lotus within my heart;
Granting then all attainments,
Both the highest, and the shared.

Nowadays a human life
Is short as lightning in the sky—
Even a long one flies,
Like the setting winter sun.
You may be alive, for now,
But don't you think
It might be better
To make some preparations
For the final end,
Instead of whatever it is
That you're doing right now?

The moment you snap
Out of sleep,
It's all the same, isn't it,
Whether you have spent
A hundred years
Or a single instant
Within that one last dream.
Life will pass,
Like an illusion
Like a bubble
Like a stroke
Of lightning.

But there is something different—
A perfect place
Beyond being born
Once more like this;
Beyond getting old;
Beyond all sickness;
Beyond death itself:
A place which instead
Stays as long as the sky.
Reach out, and you will reach it;
Reach out, while you still have the strength;
And if you miss the chance to reach
You are nothing if not
A foolish child.

Look at all of you,
Reaching for all those
Supposedly good things
Of this life;
Things that make you feel good
But never satisfy you—
Pleasure that ruins,
Hard-won at the cost
Of ignoring what might hurt others,
The pain, and others' disdain.

If you had any mind at all,
And you could see
What all this gets you,
Then what could ever keep you
From stepping into
The crystal palace
Of the three holy bodies
Of an enlightened being?
Bodies of immutable bliss,
Bodies that, when you attain them,
Shine like that Jewel
Of the daytime sky,

Banishing every trace
Of the mass of darkness:
Every bad deed ever done.

Oh you've put your heart into it;
You've read the prayers for the families,
Paid your respects, made your offerings,
And you got what you wanted:
Some kind of pleasure, here in the world—
Consolidating, investing, multiplying
All the money you made.

But maybe now those gourmet dishes
Stab like poison in your gut;
Maybe now you're more a fool
Than a fool who's paid out all his wealth
And fine gold coin for some empty hulls
Of rice sticking off a pile of shit.

Don't you recall
That thing they said
In all the open and secret books?
If you want the very quickest path
To reach the realms of misery,
Then throw yourself into secret rites
To reach money, to reach long life,
To gain power, to destroy your enemies—
All for nobody but yourself.

Friends, dear friends,
If you hope to help yourself
In any small way at all,
And if you possess
Some real intelligence—
Then can't you see that following
The path of the Brahmin Tsanakya[17]
Is like leaping eyes wide open
Off the edge of a cliff?

All this is just a little relaxing talk
Between me and those of you
Who have a good mind;
And all I have to say to you is,
"Throw off now the iron fetters
Of the eight worldly thoughts.
Stop and think, think carefully,
About what result will come to you
If you give yourself up to holy practices
Of reciting the sacred scriptures
And undertaking spiritual hardships,
Making a thousand devoted efforts
To get some worldly gain for yourself,
All of it only—for yourself." ♥

Song of the Realized Being

Namo Guru Manjughoshaya.
I bow down to my Lama, Gentle Voice.

I go for shelter,
Until the day I reach enlightenment,
At the lotus feet of my Lama,
The one who possesses all three—[18]
Every enlightened being
Of the past, present, and future,
All in a single human form.
Take me after you,
In your great love,
And never let us be apart.

Locked in unbreakable chains
Karma and my own bad thoughts
The limitless ocean
Of the wheel of pain—
Battered by the waves
Of being born, of getting old,
Of being sick, of simply dying—
The simple thought of it
Cold wind of fear
In my heart.

Gods of the world—
Pure One, Lord of Power,
Master of the World, Cruelty,
Keepers of the cup of deathlessness
Shining in your glory
Helpless dropping to lowest hell
To burn—
Who can trust
The happiness of the higher realms?

Even emperors of the wheels
Of gold and silver

Unlimited life, unlimited wealth—
But life is nothing to trust,
And again they are slaves
The lowest of slaves.
Pain, pain,
There is nothing here.

Last life's enemy, this life's family
This life's enemy, next life's friend—
The circle of life's a confusing place
The random dance of a madman. . .

Friends and relatives loved so dear
Heartloves, lovely,
Missed already a moment away—
Each time came
Each one gone
Why do you keep on hoping?

Any bad deed was acceptable
Any trouble, any disgrace
To get money,
And keep it all for me—
Helpless to carry a single atom
Along with you,
Leaving empty-handed
It hurts just to think of it.

Just a moment left
To live the rest of your life
Only a minute
For the invitation to arrive
Maybe just one touch better
Find a way to step back a bit
From the cliff
To the other side. . .

Weeping
Thinking of things you did before
A burden of sins and broken vows

Heavier than any mountain—
Nothing I hate more
Than the idea of this
One last trip—
Shaking, scared.

When I lie down that last time
On my bed, to die,
No roaring warrior
Is going to make it go away—
I can't buy it off
With every penny in the universe,
I can't buy it off
With some pretty young thing.

The Medicine Buddha,
Young King of the Healing Arts,
Can arrive himself
At that very moment—
And there's nothing he could do.
Surrounded by a crowd
Of friends I love so bad
It hurts my heart,
I will depart . . . alone . . .
I . . . am . . . afraid . . .

To walk down that narrow
Cliffside path
Of the in-between,
Ripping waves of
Hallucination
From what I did to others—
When the pain comes
When the terror itself
Actually comes
What—
Do you think
There's something
You can do then?

Oh look! I managed to collect
All they call "the good life"—
And then suddenly I drop
This sham of the body
At the side of the road—
Just one more
Abandoned house—
My mind drifts off
A fine down feather
Floating off—on the wind—
Aimless beginningless
Disease of the mind.

Caught, forced again
By how I treated others
To cross back over—
Wrapped in slime and shit
Stinking darkness in another womb—
Thinking of it
Makes my heart
Hurt . . .

There inside her belly
The shadows descend again
And I forget again what I knew
Of the holy teachings—
And again I embark
On the sheer stupidity
Of childhood—
The moral idiot
Oblivious of right or wrong . . .
Remembering how I used to be then
Enough to make me . . . mad . . .

One more time then
Through growing up
One more time through
Being grown up—
Mixing one more time
With the wrong people,

Infected by the power
Of their triple poison—
Getting things ready
One more time
For a trip to the pain
Of the lower realms
Despite myself—
I'm not really sure now
What . . . to do . . .

Tired,
So very tired,
A bucket in the bottomless well
Of pain that perpetuates itself—
Raising houses
Tearing them down
Up on the good deeds
Back down on the bad
Sometimes happy
Sometimes miserable
The ferris wheel
Of the life we lead.

Circling circling over and over
There's not a joy
There's not a pain
I haven't experienced
Over, and over,
For time with no beginning
Up to this single second—
Maybe . . . it's enough now . . .
Maybe . . . I should be . . . tired . . . of it

Look at yourself Lobsang,
Sleeping Lobsang,
Lobsang, sad thing—
Make some kind of choice
Now—
What will it be,
Happiness, or pain?

If you care about yourself
At all—
Ask yourself now,
What will you do?

I took a good look
In the crystal mirror
Of my own mind;
I saw
This world of pain
Reflected there—
All of a sudden
These words came to me,
And I put them down
On paper—
For you,
From Lobsang Chugyen. ♥

Song of a Burning Heart

Namo Guru Manjughosaya.
I bow down to my Lama, Gentle Voice.

You have reached that highest place,
The state of the triple body;
And yet to the eyes of others
You appear as a common monk.
O wisdom of the Buddhas themselves,
Lobsang Drakpa,
I beg you to come and seat yourself
Within the lotus of my heart.

Look upon me with love,
This child of yours,
A child with a rotten heart—
Someone who looks quite presentable
From the outside,
In these lovely golden robes,
But who in truth is a drunken madman,
Drunk on the wine
Of the triple poison inside his own mind—
A mangy fox hidden beneath
The golden skin of a lion.

Oh I'm perfectly aware
Of the faults within my heart—
The negative thoughts, the poisons five;[19]
But the seeds I have from living with them,
The simple habit of wrongness so strong—
And the antidote to them so fragile,
So little able to face these thoughts,
So impotent to turn them away—
There is danger
That I will burn in the realms of hell.

It had been my intent
To travel the length and breadth
Of our land

Seeing everyone and everything
As pure.
But I reached a narrow path
Along a cliffside stream—
The limits of my own motivation.
Pierced by the iron nail
Of my jealousy and pent-up anger—
There is danger
That I will slip and fall
Into the abyss
Of giving up the teachings.

Oh, I'm a true master
At explaining the Dharma,
And changing other people's minds.
And here my own mind
Remains as resistant to change
As a dry old piece of leather.
Sometimes when I teach the Dharma
I feel like an actor,
Spouting my lines by rote—
Or a parrot mindlessly repeating
Something it may have heard.
There is danger
That the one who brings you the Dharma
Will be left himself
Without a trace of it.

I had hoped to accomplish
Some practice of that deepest truth;
But I got lost in gain and fame:
To make people think I knew something
I collected all these little bits of knowledge—
There is danger
That I will miss the forest
For the trees.

What I should have done, of course,
Was to reach some feelings
Of sadness for this life—

Some desire to leave it behind.
But the great demon of thinking
That things could last
Whispered to my heart—
There is danger
That I will ignore
The warnings, the stories,
And die clawing after the things I possess—
Things outside me
Things inside me.

I had delusions
That I'd entered
The path of the greater way;
But there was a traitor in our midst—
The Butcher:
My obsession with getting
What I want.
And so here I am
With my desires, with my anger,
And better than anyone
At discriminating between everyone—
There is danger
That I will cheat my fathers
And deceive my mothers,
Every living thing
In all six realms.

I look and look
Upon the true image
Of the fact that nothing is real—
But me and my meditation seat
Are not the closest of friends.
And so instead this grasping
To things as real
Pops up pops up pops up
In my head.
There is danger
That the watchmen
Of recollection and awareness
Are off doing something else. ♥

Get Yourself to Some Wild Desert Place

Namo Guru Manjughoshaya.
I bow down to my Lama, Gentle Voice.

You are the Lord,
The very essence of the wisdom
Of every enlightened being there is.
You are my father, Lobsang Drakpa,
A father that none can compare with.
Come, o Lord of Living Kind,
And seat yourself here in the midst
Of the lotus at this one man's heart.
Grant me all the goals—
Both those of the world,
And those beyond it.

Where we live
Is here, in the terror of the prison of the cycle of pain.
Up to now
We have circled here, in birth and aging, sickness and death.
Today
My Holy Lama, look upon me with compassion.
Help me
I beg you, to stop my own karma, and the afflictions within my mind.

Youth,
This sprout of burgeoning vigor and strength
Ripens
In the end, step by step, as months turn into years.
I think
Sometimes of my younger days, the petty mind of that child,
Or else sometimes
About this decrepit body, and distaste fills my soul.

Look
On the summer meadow, that flower shining bright—
Lovely
In its exquisite form, enough to steal your heart away.

But by the time
The moon has made its appearance high,
Its color
Is faded . . . it withers . . . to ugliness itself.

Aren't we
Just the same? At first so lovely to look upon—
Youth
Arrogant, bedecked in the jewels of health and strength.
But by the end
Here we are, our time used up, the body old and weak—
Disgusting
To look upon, nothing more than a walking corpse.

Inside
The power of flesh and blood has waned;
Outside
The skin hangs now in baggy flaps—
A mass
Of wrinkles draws checkerboards across my body,
However much
I try to sit up straight, the back bends like a bow.

The roots
Of those pretty little tooth-trees rotted, and they fell out.
The branches
Of my lips tremble in the wind, but it's no pretty sight.
When I talk
It comes out all garbled, no one can make it out.
Down my chin
Run little dribbles of saliva, all unnoticed.

When I try to stand up,
I need hands and feet both, to push the ground away.
When I try to sit down,
It feels like I'm taking a massive pack off my back.
This little table
Of the legs and thighs and those small little toes
Can no longer support
The weight of that box—my body—so everything starts to shake.

Most of my hair
Has fallen out, and what's left has turned to gray;
My eyes
Are blurry, they've sounded retreat, and sunken back in my head.
When people talk
To me, or I to them, the guards at my ears make fast the gates;
My mind's
Gone stupid, I can't remember anything, all my powers have faded.

I'm doing my best
To hold this corpse up with my cane,
But when I walk
I can only shuffle along—at times I fall.
Now most
Of my life is used up
I've almost reached the other side—

Now even my friends
And loved ones, followers and helpers are starting to say,
"It's got to the point
Where he might be better off dead"—to pray for me to die!
I'm old, I'm old,
All the strength of life is gone—
The inside
Of the trunk of this tree has rotted away.

And the terror
Of having to go through all this
Is not just something
That's happened to me this one time alone—
I've seen it
Over and over, in an unbroken stream of lives.

And the way
You've seen how I've gotten old and fallen apart
Comes to each
And every one of us, by the very nature of things.
But you
Children in the bloom of your youth

Are blissfully unaware
Of all this, still hoping that health lasts forever.

Oh you can paint
This pile of shit and piss with a layer of gold
And think it's pretty,
But soon enough the truth will out.
The longbow of
The Lord of Power paints a shining picture across the sky,[20]
But the sheen
Of life so quickly fades away.

And so now,
When you've gotten together the body that you need,
Go the forest
Of medicine trees, to that lovely garden of delights,
And pick yourself
Some of what's there: master the twelve-count practice,[21]
Read the accounts found
In those high open and secret books of the Word.

Listen to as many
Teachings as you can, and contemplate their deepest points;
Go and have a good time
Playing in their meaning, in the single-pointed bliss of meditation.
Later on you can walk
In the footsteps of those who—after it happens—see the illusion.
And take some time sometimes
To go off wandering by yourself in the wide-open mountains.

Go all the way
From the steps of the path that are shared with others
To the glory
Of greatest bliss, in the union of the two.
Sit yourself down
On a single seat—concentrate everything there.
Take joy
In meditating round the clock, night and day.

By the end
You may find that your youth has gone full circle,
But everything will turn out
Just as the king, the all-knowing Lord of the Able, has said:
"If a monk
Has taken themselves and mastered many teachings,
Then there's nothing
More pleasant for them than whiling their life away
In the delightful garden
That you find in the midst of a simple wild forest."
You can believe
What he said: you'll never need fear old age or death.

Rip the roots
Of the eight worldly worries out of your mind;
Get yourself to some
Wild desert place, which will turn out for you the garden of gods.
Surrender yourself gladly
To repeating the life that your father, your Lama, has already led.

Above, the silent gliding clouds are for you
The gold silk canopy over the throne of a master Teacher.
A bit farther down
Is the woodland mist, which you can use as your upper robe.
Below that stand the lovely
Green plants of the forest, a perfect lower robe you can wear.
For the earth below that holds
All this up, there's a verdant meadow covered in poppies.
And for trouble-free friends
You will always have your birds, and other wild creatures.

You may find yourself
Dancing in happiness, now that your mind is put to ease;
No one even to mention the names
Of friends and relatives and enemies and all—
All the people
You've wasted this life on to love and to hate.

You have come now
To the forest of magical medical trees,

And here you are free from the pain
Of getting and protecting money, or of not having any at all.
Little things might pop up,
But you will be sustained by the deathless nectar of simplicity.
The only accounts you need to manage now
Are the seven riches of those who've seen emptiness.

Whatever work
You might have to do, your only boss is you.
Train yourself then,
Follow in the deeds of every Lord and Victor.
They say that
The special kind of happiness which comes
From this way of life
Is something rare for even the kings of the gods.

So be like a golden duck
Flying high in the sky, who spots then far away
A wishing-giving lake
Covered over in lovely lotus lace—
Look ahead
To your garden of bliss, your wild desert home.

Go now quickly
Into the wilderness, go so you can be free
Of this endless
Bottomless sea—the pain of the circle of life,
Where packs
Of sharks attack you: your karma, your negative thoughts;
And mountainous waves
Crash down on you—your birth, old age, your sickness and death.

Use the deep practice,
The path that combines method and wisdom,
To rip out the hearts
Of your enemies: that birth, that aging, the sickness and death.
In every moment of your life
Pray for a body and things and friends that no longer come and go.

By the power
Of my Lama and the Triple Gem, which cannot ever fail,
May we quickly attain
All the deep goals we hope for—all those expressed in these lines.
May every obstacle
That might keep them from coming true soon be stopped,
And every
Helpful condition that might give them birth soon appear. ♥

The Dance of the Daughter

Look at that!

Strange, isn't it—
To look at the knowing
And invisible mind,
Starting but never stopping,
And realize
That it couldn't have started at all.
The sensual dance
Of the daughter
Of a barren woman—
A thing that never stays,
Having never started
And never either to end.

The mind
Completely devoid of the extreme, some pretend reality
Its dance
Never ending shining shining brightness conscious
A realm
Liberation free of the grasping fingers of held and holder
In this moment
How could it be, that I hold now the end?

He gets others
To meditate on the teachings of emptiness, and the great seal—
But he himself
Never meditates, and there's nothing he meditates on—
There's not the slightest
Sign that he's meditated on a single atom of this truth—
Go ahead,
Meditate all you want, practice all you want . . .

Now there's not
The slightest difference, whether I live or die—
This mind now
Will forever live its life in the company of a higher friend—

Never again apart
From what seems, what's void, from supreme ecstasy—
Go ahead,
Make all the pain you want, all the pain you want.

O you logicians
Men of words, with eyes that only point to the outside,
You will read these words,
And find here a mountain of disallowable paradox—
But if there's some yogi
Who has any actual experience of the thing itself,
I know
This song of mine will bring a little smile to her lips. ♥

Rainbow Arching over the Path to Deathlessness

Namo Guru Manjughoshaya.
I bow down to my Lama, Gentle Voice.

Your holy form—
Just to lay eyes upon its blazing light
Means I've done at least one important thing
With my life.

And what you say—
Roaring with the sweet music
Possessed of sixty high qualities.

Your sacred mind—
Gone beyond the cycle, gone beyond peace,
A goldmine of knowledge and love.

O Lord,
The one who holds the diamond,
I bow myself down at your lotus feet.

Driven
By that demon, the great mistake
Of grasping onto things,
My mind
Makes up different objects
Where none exist, and craves them.
The force
Of that then makes me divide
What I see as "me," and see as "you."
The power
Of my bad thoughts and the deeds I do
Then send me wandering through the cycle.

But now
I wield the razor sword
Of realizing how all this works.

If I don't
Use it now to take the life
Of my foe, this holding on to some self,
Then the pain
That I go through here in this place,
This ocean of the cycle of terror,
Will circle
Round in circles again,
Never a moment's respite.

This mind
Of mine, this machine of illusion,
This misunderstanding of things,
Suddenly saw
That the things it was looking at
Had never begun at all.
And then
I suddenly dropped into the realm
Below all ideas of held and holder—
It was like
Falling through a layer of ice,
Into the great salt sea.

I looked upon
The very face of every existing thing,
The way things are since they ever were;
A thing
Torn from every idea I'd had of it,
All things melded to one—
A realm
Of existence where the nature of things
Compared to one thing, nothing;
And in the moment
That I looked, and saw
The thing I saw,

I realized
That even the simple names
Of our Lords—the Buddhas,
The Dharma,

And the Community—
Were things that could never be.
And once
You've seen how this mind,
This misunderstanding poisons things,
Then how
Could you ever again feel pain
Here in the cycle of life?

Put your mind
Into that ultimate object:
Into the simple state of clear light.
See the essence
Of every single thing there is,
And see it face-to-face.
If you look
A second time, you'll see
It was never anything to see.
Look, if you like,
For the very end
Of the never-ending sky.

Seek
The awesome vision wherein
Every single living being
Terrified
By the cycle of life
Now rests in bliss and emptiness.
See this,
And you will never again
Feel the least bit of fear,
Even if
All these apparent people
Should become your sworn enemy.

Karma—
The fruits of good and evil deeds
Never existed at all.
The path—
Things to stop, things to stop them,

Reaching, avoiding, never happened.
The mind—
Is completely void of all those goals
You worked so hard to attain.
This . . . place—
It seems to me
Is what the Victors wanted to teach us.

I set my gaze
Still further out, at all the things
In the cycle of pain, and beyond.
And because of this
I thought I saw some cause and effect
That was infinitely more subtle;
Something
That no matter what
Would never turn out wrong.
It was like
A rainbow arching over
The path to deathlessness.

It was
A realm free of any ideas,
Pure from the very beginning--
It was
A place where karma,
Cause and effect, never could go wrong—
It was
A world where the apparent world
And emptiness no longer alternated—
It was
A truth, a middle path, free of extremes,
The union of the two.

The fact
That I have found this path
Is the kindness of my Lama.
Kindness
Great, great Lord, a second
Victorious Buddha come to the world.

Give then
Your blessing now, that all
These mother beings of kindness
May also
Come to lay their eyes
Upon this ultimate truth. ♥

The Union of the Two

Namo Guru Manjughoshaya.
I bow down to my Lama, Gentle Voice.

You are
The realm, the path of the gods,
Knowledge that is inseparable.
You are
The paradise, you are everywhere,
The sacred dance of illusion.
You are
My father, a father that was never real,
As real as a father in a dream.
I am
Your son, I am a person
Who is no more real than some illusion.

And I bow to you
From my very heart.

No matter what I look at
It looks like nothing more
Than an illusion.
Even when I look at
This way things really are,
I can't see anything.
Oh yes, and now I've found
The union of the two—
That path where the illusion
And emptiness are joined as one.
And I've found it through
The kindness of my Lama.
A la la!
Don't go off one side
And think that things are there;
Don't go off the other side
And think that they are not—

Stay and meditate
In the realm of emptiness,
Where neither side is there.

When you look
At the way things really are,
The thing you're looking at
Finally comes clear.
But then when you check
This very same thing,
Your mind retreats
Into emptiness.
There is a place though,
The union of the two,
Where the way things appear
And their sheer emptiness
No longer alternate, back and forth.
And I've found that place,
Through my Lama's kindness.
A la la!
Don't go off one side
And think that things are there;
Don't go off the other side
And think that they are not—
Stay and meditate
In the realm of emptiness,
Where neither side is there.

Ultimate reality
Comes and teaches me
That things happen
In a cause and effect
That never goes
The slightest bit wrong.
Deceptive reality
Comes and parts
The veil which covers
Ultimate reality.
There is a place,
The union of the two,

Where these two realities
Share the very same nature,
Inseparable one from the other.
And I've found that place,
Through my Lama's kindness.
A la la!
Don't go off one side
And think that things are there;
Don't go off the other side
And think that they are not—
Stay and meditate
In the realm of emptiness,
Where neither side is there.

When I really look into
This empty realm
Of ultimate reality,
Then I see that even the name
"Dependent origination"
Was never even there.
There is a place,
The union of the two,
Where emptiness and dependence
Are completely compatible—
And I've found that place,
Through my Lama's kindness.
A la la!
Don't go off one side
And think that things are there;
Don't go off the other side
And think that they are not —
Stay and meditate
In the realm of emptiness,
Where neither side is there.

Come to realize
That not a single thing
In the entire universe,
Not a thing in the cycle of pain,
And not a thing beyond it,

Has any reality at all.
With this then you know the truth.
But there is a place,
A union of the two,
Where what is real and what is false
Are completely indivisible.
And I've found that place,
Through my Lama's kindness.
A la la!
Don't go off one side
And think that things are there;
Don't go off the other side
And think that they are not—
Stay and meditate
In the realm of emptiness,
Where neither side is there.

Things are nothing more than names
Things are void of any reality at all
And the fact that nothing is real
Dances in every cause and effect—
And I've found that path,
Where emptiness, and cause and effect,
Can never again be parted.
Eh ma ho!
I found it through my Lama's kindness—
Ah la la!
I've stepped back from the cliff
Of thinking things will last forever;
I've stepped back from the cliff
Of thinking they have stopped. ♥

Naked, Dressed in the Robe of Emptiness

Namo Guru Manjughoshaya.
I bow down to my Lama, Gentle Voice.

I bow
To the master of magical illusion,
Who can make
Anything appear at all:
The realm
Beyond all words,
And the ecstasy
Coupled to it.
He is
My father, my Lama, my Lord,
The one
Who holds the diamond.
I bow
To your feet, to the one who steals away
The terror
Of this cycle of pain, this enemy of mine.

It was today
That a great many different
And amazing
Sketches appeared within my mind
About the dance
Of the things that appear around me —
Things
That seem to contradict each other
When in actuality
They are in no contradiction at all.
I'll set down
In writing just a tiny fraction
Of what I saw,
In this song of a realized being.

I looked out
At every object that appeared to me,
And understood
That it was all false, nothing on its own.
When I understood,
Then the truth showed its face to me.
It was my mind,
Naked, dressed in the robe of emptiness.

Every single
Thing there is—the two separate sides,
The source
Of pain, and total enlightenment—
Was mixed together
Inseparably, in that highest realm there is.
It was the path
Where there was nothing to prove or disprove,
But still
That oh-so-wise mind of mine
Saw how right
The laws of karma are: what to do, and what not.

The first thing I did
Was to spot my enemy, my grasping to myself;
I struck at its heart
With the sharp sword of scripture and reasoning.
Now when I look
In that vast mirror where nothing can be seen,
I still see a me
That I see in a way where nothing is seen.

When I look
On all the things there are, nothing stands on anything.
When I look
On the object of the way things are, everything appears.
I have a path,
Vast, truth, the union of appearances and emptiness.
Everything there is
Is tightly bound now, in the ropes of this same way.

All is beyond
Being one, or being many;
And yet
In the realm of the single song
It is once more
One, dancing as the many.
Seek some image
You can use to picture it: something no one can do.
I want so much
To tell you the essence, of the thing that cannot be told.

The world
We want to rid ourselves of doesn't exist at all.
The path
For reaching freedom is a simple impossibility.
And yet the pain
Of all my mothers is unbearable, unbearable.
Let me now attain,
Quickly now, the three forms of the divine. ♥

Regarding the Compositions ࿐

This section contains brief excerpts describing the personal, political, or historical circumstances surrounding His Holiness as he composed each of these beautiful, heartfelt verses. By referencing these comments alongside their associated poem, one may fully understand each verse. Comments by the translators are in italic, and Yongdzin Yeshe Gyeltsen's explanatory text from the *Brief Biography* is presented in regular type.

The Lady Who Came to Me

At the age of 14, His Holiness the First Panchen Lama already sees his Angel. This is the story of that first meeting, in 1584. It is taken from pp. 493-495 in A Brief Biography of His Holiness the First Panchen Lama, Lobsang Chukyi Gyeltsen, *written by Tsechok Ling, Yongdzin Yeshe Gyeltsen.*

This poetry is extraordinary even by tantric standards. It is written in the high classical style of Sanskrit, and also includes—in Tibetan—a great many of the classical metaphors of ancient India. For example, even in just the first few lines, "Blue Lord" is an unusual, literal translation of the Sanskrit word for sapphire; and the "child of the lake" refers to a lotus. This latter word, and many other words in the poem, have hidden, tantric meanings as well.

To put it simply, we can't expect to grasp every subtlety of His language here. But the incredible, divine, and surreal sense of the English is exactly what the Tibetan feels like. It must be some of the greatest poetry ever written in Tibetan— all by a teenager.

On the eighth day of that same month, he came to that wise and accomplished master, Kedrup Sangye Yeshe, and had the good fortune to be granted the rite of permission into the secret world of the Lady of Song (*Sarasvati,* or *Yangchenma*), in her form of purest white.

Beginning on the tenth day he went into a retreat, for seven days, to reach Her. And then he met Her, face to face, this Lady of Song in Her ivory form, the one woman of every Victor, the Lady known as "The Goddess of Words and Melody."

Here is what he saw. Out of the heart of the Lady of Song comes another goddess, another Lady of Song—this one with a body of sea-blue green. In her two hands she bears forth a priceless bowl of jewel, filled with fresh fruit that are, in reality, high spiritual attainments in a physical form. This Lady of the Sky turns, and offers the bowl and its fruit to the first Lady.

The Lady reaches forth Her right hand, and accepts one of the pieces of fruit. From within this fruit appears yet another goddess: the Princess of the Pure One, in a body of crimson light. She lifts the bowl and its fruit out of the hands of the Lady of Song, and turns, and offers it to our Lord. He takes a piece, and partakes of it.

And in that moment he pretends to first step through the door to the wisdom of the treasure of the sky. In this life, he has yet to engage in any study of the art of composing scripture; and yet in-between sessions of this same retreat a strong desire is born in his heart to write a poem in praise of the Goddess, the Lady of Song, to describe how She has come to him.

And in that same instant, the lines come to him, all in wave of vision, and he sets down the verses.

This poem was found as a handwritten manuscript. Since it sings the praises of the Lady of Song according to someone who is describing what they actually saw, the great masters who are spiritual sons of the venerable Lobsang Chukyi Gyeltsen speak as one in referring to it as *The Praise of the Lady of Song, Who Came to Me.*

A Love-Poem to my Buddha Lama

His Holiness the First Panchen Lama is already a mature teacher, about 40 years old, by the time of our next episode in his life, recounted in Yongdzin Yeshe Gyeltsen's brief biography at pp. 510-511. Here he recalls the kindness of the Teacher.

He went then to Trashi Hlunpo—the monks there were in the traditional monk's summer retreat. He separated them into groups of 25 each, and then group by group he took them to the main temple, and granted them an extensive tantric empowerment into the Angel known as Parasol of White.

After the traditional opening of the summer retreat, he went into a retreat for 21 days. His main subject of meditation was the sutra known as *Close Recollection upon the Jewels*. He made great efforts in collecting new good karma, and cleaning away old bad karma.

And then he had an extraordinary experience of overwhelming faith, thinking of all the incredible kindness that our Teacher, Lord Buddha, the Compassion One, has showered upon us all. The supplication, *A Cry of Heart-Rending Faith,* came to him.

The Death of a Disciple

In this selection, His Holiness is already in his late forties; for years now he has been cultivating the young Fourth Dalai Lama, His Holiness Yunten Gyatso, and has just presided over his ordination. His Holiness the First Panchen Lama suddenly loses, to the Lord of Death, a number of disciples that he had trained at length, with hopes that they would pass on the teachings. These include the young Dalai Lama; and the Panchen Lama weeps in a poem. The Death of a Disciple, *at pp. 527-528 in Yongdzin Yeshe Gyeltsen's* Brief

Biography. *The following event speak for themselves in reminding us to contemplate our coming death.*

In that same year [1615], he was able to accomplish the ordination of many hundreds of people into the vows of a full monk. These groups were headed by such illustrious high reincarnated Lamas as Tunkor Trulku Jamyang Gyatso and Kyishu Shabdrung Tendzin Lobsang Gyatso.

He returned then to Trashi Hlunpo. There he bestowed the empowerments of the *Diamond Garland* and the *Collection of Mitra* to a group of over 300 scholars of the Three Baskets, headed by the two above-mentioned Lamas, as well as the Master of Surshi.

He was requested then by groups of the Tse House of Trashi Hlunpo to teach there, and he granted a great many teachings, including the great initiations into the three tantras of the *Secret Collection (Guhyasamaja), Greatest Bliss (Heruka),* and *the Frightener (Bhairava);* as well as rites of permission for the practices of a great many Dharma protectors.

At that time in his life, many of his direct disciples, whom he had cultivated with great hopes that they would be of benefit to the teachings, began to die without warning, one after the other. Then, in the twelfth month of the year of golden red—which is to say, the fire snake year [1617]—the Omniscient Yunten Gyatso suddenly passed on to another realm, sending his holy mind to its final rest within the ether of all things.

At this same moment, the First Panchen Lama was presiding over the Great Prayer Festival in Lhasa. As soon as the Prayer was ended, he went immediately to the monastery of Radreng, and threw himself into deep retreat. A strong realization of impermanence was born in his heart. A song came to him then.

Laughing in the Dark, a Song of Sadness

His Holiness the First Panchen Lama is about 40 years old in this excerpt from Yongdzin Yeshe Gyeltsen's Brief Biography, *at pp. 511-512. Here he laments the circumstances of life, pain, and the lower realms.*

In the second month of that autumn then he traveled to Chenlung. He was able to induce many hundreds of people to commit themselves to taking one-day vows; and undertaking spiritual fasts; giving up the act of killing; and reciting mantras or the like. More particularly, he went to Kachu in Chenlung and granted the entire four empowerments of the divine being Unmoving, in the teachings of the *Secret Collection*—as well as many other Dharma teachings that people desired.

And so he traveled from Nyangtu down south, through Tsakok, and all the way to Chenlung. Wherever he went, a crowd would suddenly spring up, as if market day had come—and then before long it was always time to leave them again. He saw people at each place, a lot of people, who had been torn by death from beloved family or friends; they came with tears in their eyes, asking him to say prayers for the dead.

"Look at them," he said, crying in pity. "Look— here are some in the prime of youth, well-built, flirting with one another. And here are others in their middle age; and others who are old, on the verge of death." Many were living without a care in the world; laughing, thinking of nothing. The great majority of them were making offerings to the Lord himself, giving things that they had accumulated out of their unwillingness to share with others, hoping they would get something out of it.

> Forget about the cycle of pain;
> forget about what's been happen-
> ing for time with no beginning.
> Just look at them here and now,
> in this one short life. The situa-
> tion with family and friends goes
> up, and then down. These great
> crowds of people who come to
> see me, these people in the prime
> of their youth, it's all as brief as a
> rainbow in the sky.
>
> And these things they bring to
> offer me—all these things they've
> accumulated by refusing to share
> with others—they're all just a trap,
> like sticky honey inside a bee hive.
> Oh everything around me is my
> Teacher, showing me very clearly,
> right to my face, how life really is.

And so out of sadness in his holy heart, he wrote this song of his own experience.

Begging the Buddha for Shelter

His Holiness the First Panchen Lama is already over 65 years old by the time this piece is written. There has been major bloodshed in the country for some years, and more is on its way—this time with monks involved in the fighting. Late in His life and surrounded by bloodshed, His Holiness the First Panchen Lama cries out to the Buddha to help us. He cries for shelter in this selection from Yongdzin Yeshe Gyeltsen's Brief Biography, *at pp. 552-553.*

There were at that time in particular a great many figures who had delusions of grandeur, seeking power—they caused disturbances in the land, and the people were pushed down into misery. He saw that he had no direct means to help these deluded ones, and that brought him great sadness. Out of pain and compassion then he wrote these words of supplication to the Jewels.

A Song of Sadness at the State of My Mind

His Holiness the First Panchen Lama detects his own lower motivation even for good deeds, such as teaching others the Dharma, in this reflection upon karma and it's consequences. The title and the song speak for themselves in this excerpt fromYongdzinYeshe Gyeltsen's Brief Biography, *at pp. 513-514.*

Because these incidents were unlimited in number, I shall not write here any description of how—over the course of his life—he received various offerings from the many people who had faith in him, and how he utilized this offerings to help construct temples, or to support and honor the spiritual community.

At the insistent request of the masters of Trashi Hlunpo, he granted the entire initiation into the four empowerments of the glorious secret teaching of the *Diamond Frightener—Vajra Bhairava*—within the secret world of colored sand.

As soon as the summer monks' retreat let out, he went into isolation for three weeks, concentrating on gaining actual experiential realizations of the various stages of the path. During this time, the following thoughts were passing through his divine mind:

Up to now people have been calling me a lama—but the whole time I've been helpless, controlled by other thoughts, everything mixed up with the eight worldly attitudes.

I have accepted money and things from the faithful—from hands with fingernails both white and red[22] —and from the belongings of the deceased as well. And sometimes I wonder if I haven't just wasted them all.

I have helped build temples and shrines and the like, to the absolute limits of my capacity; and I've taught the Dharma too, giving initiations and oral transmissions and explanations and all the rest, supposedly for the sake of the teachings, and other people. But I can hardly claim that I did so filled with any thoughts of renunciation, or correct worldview.

And the fact is that I may engage in a great many acts of impure virtue this way—good karma that is not imbued with renunciation and worldview—but all these actions will do then is to keep me circling around in the cycle of pain.

I may perhaps be able to get some nice things in this life, but still it's unbearable to remain here even for a moment, smothered in the flame of all this pain and worry— taking birth, getting old, dying again.

For me to say that this pain is unbearable, and then to sit here, making no great effort to escape from these five great terrors[23], is sad, sad...ah, it must be that my heart is made of stone—or perhaps I really am insane.

He saw with his own holy eyes then how each and every good thing that we can ever get here in the cycle of pain is, in its essence, simply pain. And so then he composed the *Song of the Aryas*.

While We Still Have Some Choices Left

A poem on trying to establish the desire to reach nirvana, with accompanying historical material at pp. 503-504 in the Brief Biography.

During this period of his life [His Holiness is about 60 years old at this point] he began to develop an intense attraction to going out to very remote areas for his practice. He was thinking to himself as follows:

Now I'm going to devote myself to the spiritual austerity of giving up all eternal activity. And in this endeavor I will remain completely unstoppable, just like the great spiritual adepts of olden days.

But to succeed at this, I'll have to sever myself completely from the tentacles of this present life: this tendency to think of nothing but nice clothes and good food.

It would be a bad thing if I were to
become a hermit only in name, just a
wild animal that lives on its own.

And so he trained himself in a great many forms of
the practice of living off nothing but the tiny essential
parts of plants, and kept this up continually. He had
long since mastered the yogic practices of breath con-
trol and the physical poses of the Machine of the Body;
but now to boost their effect he waited until the snows
began and then traveled to Drakgya for retreat. Here
within the length of seven days he was able to accom-
plish the Kagyu practice where you need wear nothing
more than a light piece of cloth, even in such conditions.

Here in retreat he had no distractions at all, and so
his holy mind became even more crystal clear than
ever before. He began to sing a great many songs
about his personal spiritual experiences, some of
which he set down in writing. Here is one.

Admission into Agony

*His Holiness the First Panchen Lama is already in his sixties
when he composes this poem reflecting his own despair over
the very nature of this impure world and all it's sufferings. It
has been a time of turmoil and sectarian violence in Tibet,
and we feel his sadness over the very nature of the cycle of
pain, which we too are living in.* Admission into Agony, *at
pp. 551-552 in Yongdzin Yeshe Gyeltsen's* Brief Biography.

In those hard days he wrote a great many spiritual
songs, moved by fierce feelings of despair about the
state of the world. Here is one of them.

The Killer Child

*His Holiness the First Panchen Lama is in his thirties when
he writes this denunciation of his own negative emotions and*

*the role they play in the chain of suffering. He pretends to
have a sudden realization that it is the negative emotions
within his own heart which are the great enemy of an entire
lifetime, and more, and composes this spiritual song about
personal practice describing how to get out of suffering. The
selection is once again taken from Master Tsechok Ling's*
Brief Biography, *at pp. 514-515.*

In those days too he gave a lot of thought to this short
human life—fleeting as a winter's day—reflecting
that, even if we feel happy for a while, it never actu-
ally satisfies us; whereas, even if we feel sad for a
while, it's never really the end of things.

And he was thinking about what it is to have an
enemy: I mean, a really serious enemy would be
someone who appeared in the midst of this brief life
and somehow threatened your body, your life itself,
your various possessions.

But then, he was thinking to himself, there is
another kind of enemy—the kind who takes up a bat-
tlesword of red-hot steel, and chops away at you with
it, inflicting this constant stream of misery; being
forced to take birth, and then get old, and sick and in
the end simply to die—over and over again, in a
never-ending flow within the cycle of pain, a cycle
with no beginning, an uninterrupted circle of flame on
a pitch-black night, when you take a torch and spin it
round quickly in the dark.

And he realized then suddenly that this second
enemy—the one holding the sword—was none other
than the three poisons: the negative emotions within
his very heart. It occurred to him that no other
enemy—no one in this present life, nor anyone that
ever came later—could ever compare in the slightest
that way to that inner enemy.

Here was fear, here was terror. Here was the very
source of all the pain that exists: a murderer in your
own home, posing as one of your own children. But

now he had exposed the killer; now he knew who was really in charge of ruining his life.

And so he set about the task of leveling these emotions—of cutting them down, one by one. In this spirit as well he wrote this song of a realized being.

Ready to Die, or Live

In this selection of the First Panchen Lama's poetry, he responds to repeated warnings by seers that powerful, unseen forces are threatening his life, and that counteractive rituals must be undertaken immediately. His reaction, in a nutshell, is another kind of equanimity: a person who has done all they can for their entire life to live that life well is completely ready to live or to die.

Here we see how his unshakable sense of equanimity has extended not only to other people, but to things and events as well. His Holiness the First Panchen Lama is about fifty years old in this excerpt from Yongdzin Yeshe Gyeltsen's Brief Biography, *at pp. 521-522.*

These exquisite verses are written in the same distinctive meter as the songs of the great yogi Milarepa, who lived about 500 years before the first Panchen Rinpoche. In this meter in Tibetan, the first syllable or two of each line is designed to jump out at the reader immediately—and we have tried to maintain this feeling in the English.

In those days a great many seers came forth and warned him that powerful forces were at work which could cut short his time on this earth. They implored him, saying that the traditional rituals for assuring the long and healthy life of a Lama must quickly be performed. He replied to them with this poem, about gaining a sense of equanimity in the face of the Eight Worldly Thoughts.

What Think You?

His Holiness the First Panchen Lama is about 65 years old when he writes this piece of motherly advice; a brief lam-rim in itself really, from Yongdzin Yeshe Gyeltsen's Brief Biography, *at pp. 549-550.*

In those days he composed a great many songs of his spiritual life. Here is one of them.

One Day, in a Moment of Clarity

These are perhaps some of the most incredible and extraordinary verses that His Holiness the First Panchen Lama ever wrote. The Song of the Diamond, *an almost bashful admission of high tantric realizations he had one day, which he shares "only to let others know it works," and to repay all the kindness. His Holiness is in his mid-forties in this excerpt, which is taken from Master Tsechok Ling's* Brief Biography, *at pp. 525-527.*

He traveled on then to Trashi Hlunpo, where the *rab-jampas* or master scholars of the monastery's tantric college were devoting themselves to teaching and learning the high practices of the *Secret Collection*. At this point, he also introduced into the curriculum the teaching and study of both the root tantras and commentaries upon the glorious *Kalachakra*, or *Wheel of Time*.

Following this he went into a personal retreat for some time, devoting himself single-mindedly to the practice of the Five Stages, a profound path within the teachings of the glorious *Secret Collection*. As a result, he gained high realizations into these stages. He then burst forth with the following *Song of the Diamond*. It is meant to declare the fact that there really does exist, here in the teachings of Lord Tsongkapa, a shortcut for achieving the Combination of the Two–tantric Buddhahood—in but this one brief life.

The song tells the story of how he himself succeeded in actually using this shortcut; and he writes it specifically for future generations of disciples who hope to practice in the footsteps of our Lama, the Gentle Protector, Je Tsongkapa.

Father and Son

It was the Indian master Lord Atisha (982-1054 AD) who risked his life on a long and dangerous sea voyage to Indonesia, in order to bring back the missing instructions on developing the Wish for enlightenment. He then successfully translated to Tibet the combined lineages for both the Wish and the worldview of emptiness, with the help of his devoted Tibetan heart-disciple Dromtun Je Gyalway Jungne (1005-1064). The two teamed up to bring some of the first teachings on the Wish for enlightenment to Tibet.

Dromtun Je is famous as an example of someone who never himself became a monk, but who rather as a layman succeeded in the highest practices. Without Dromtun Je's extraordinary devotion and special skills in arranging every kind of logistical support—from horses to yak butter to bricks—then his Teacher's mission in Tibet, and particularly the founding of the great Radreng Monastery, never would have happened. Dromtum Je's way of always showing up in the right place at the right time with whatever Lord Atisha needed for his work at the moment brought later generations of Tibetans to recognize that he was, in fact, a tantric deity in disguise.

And so they have set an example for us to follow: masters of The Wish—a teacher and disciple so close and with such love that they are often simply called "The Father and Son." In this pair of "love poems" to Lord Atisha and Dromtun Je, we get a clear sense of the vision that His Holiness the First

Panchen Lama had that Buddhism could and should be prac-
ticed actively and successfully not just by monks and nuns, but
by laypeople like Dromtun Je: by intelligent people with a
normal career and family life.

His Holiness The first Panchen Lama celebrates their life
with these poems, written in his 48th year and excerpted
again from Master Tsechok Ling's Brief Biography, *at pp.*
528-530.

As soon as the Munlam festival ended, he made his
way to Radreng Monastery. He went into a strict per-
sonal retreat for a month in the hills above the
monastery.

He had arranged for the precious statue of Lord
Atisha known as "A Tilt of the Head" to be brought to
him there. He made single pointed supplications to
this image, and received extraordinary signs that he
had won its blessings. As a result, he set down in writ-
ing certain verses of supplication to both the
Lord—The Father—and his spiritual Son.

The Joy of Empty Sadness

A haunting piece of spiritual poetry from His Holiness the
First Panchen Lama in which he balances the sadness which
overwhelms him when he looks at the world, and the joy he
feels when he sees its emptiness. His Holiness is about 40 years
old when he writes this piece, on the sadness of the lives of the
people around us, and the joy of its emptiness. Taken again
from Master Tsechok Ling's Brief Biography, *at pp. 518.*

In this way then he perceived, with those holy eyes,
both the way in which all existing things appear and
the way in which they really are—whether they be
included within the cycle of pain, or already beyond
it. When he looked upon the world as it appears to us,
he had a sudden and spontaneous sense of compassion
for every living being. And when he perceived the way

in which all things really are, then deep feelings of joy instantly welled up in his heart. All this led him to write a small song of his inner life.

The Peacemaker

Throughout the history of Buddhism there has been a tendency towards the image of a hermit in a cave who attains happiness by refusing to engage in the world at all. But the ideal of the bodhisattva, of the Mahayana or Greater Way, allows quite well for a hermit who enjoys deep retreat and then again emerges into society, ready and strengthened by their inner practice to help in the external affairs of the world.

In this sense, His Holiness the First Panchen Lama provides an exquisite role model that has rarely been equaled in the history of Tibet—only by such figures as Je Tsongkapa himself and, of course, by the greatest Dalai Lama of them all: our own, The Fourteenth. The Panchen Rinpoche stepped up and took personal responsibility, even in "big" situations which most of us would claim are beyond our ability to affect personally. The Panchen Lama is about 42 years old now.

This poem and historical sketch demonstrate the First Panchen Rinpoche's extraordinary sense of personal responsibility in both the spiritual life and the outside world. An eloquent and real example for all of us to follow in our own times. Excerpted from Yongdzin Yeshe Gyeltsen's Brief Biography *at pp. 524-525 and pp. 535-536.*

Gradually then he reached all the way to the Bhutanese areas of Padro, Timbu, and Darkar. The southerners who lived here—the people called the Mun—had an even greater tendency than other people to stick with their own local religious beliefs and Lamas. Our Lord though had spent his whole life without any feelings of religious prejudice: he had always tried to see the divine in the beliefs of all peoples. And because of this karma, all those that he visited paid homage to him: the respect and support he received were immeasurable.

The Lord on his part too took great pains to present all the groups of monks there with material support, and personal offerings of money to each one. With gifts of the Dharma too he showered them, bestowing upon everyone whatever teaching they happened to want—a whole range of different subjects such as the empowerments and accompanying instructions for the glorious *Secret Collection,* the *Frightener,* and other tantric deities; as well as the rites of permission for a great number of close Angels and Dharma protectors.

Townspeople too would assemble by the thousands to hear him teach. In some cases he granted them the empowerments of long life, although mainly he used this as an opportunity to teach people about the principles of karma and its consequences. He would grant the transmission of the six-syllable mantra and then urge his listeners to make some kind of pledge to follow an ethical life. Hundreds of people came forth to commit themselves to undertake spiritual fasts.

Others made commitments to recite, on a daily basis, some special prayers or the like—be it just once or 21 times, or whatever. These would include prayers like *Excellent Deeds;* or *The Prayer of Loving One;* or *The Confession of Transgressions; Verses in Praise of Tara; The Heart Sutra; The Verse for Taking Refuge;* the lines of supplication for whichever Lama they happened to follow; or even just the *mani* mantra. Others promised to give up taking any kind of life, or else to perform a certain number of prostrations—either the regular kind, or the type where you go all the way on the ground and stretch out your entire body.

As for the duration of these commitments, he induced the most serious people to promise to continue this daily practice for the rest of their lives;

whereas those who were least serious he would have commit themselves for a year. You can hardly imagine then the numbers of people who swore some kind of oath like this; and so wherever the Lord set his feet, there sprang up a whole tradition of observing moral commitments. Thus did he reveal to the common man how to lead a good life.

There were in particular people going around killing hundreds and even thousands of persons in the strife between the Gung and the Wang. Major acts of vengeance then were being planned as well, and none of these people's Lamas were doing anything to try to restrain them. And so he went himself to many of those who were intent on reprisals. He would start off by making substantial presents of money or whatever to them, and by the end he would be holding his sacred rosary to the tops of their heads, as they swore an oath that they would abandon their plans of retaliation. In this way he was able to stop the cycle of bad karma at its root, and bring a gentle atmosphere of peace to this entire southern region, the home of the Mun.

These then are typical of the ways in which he undertook great deeds of benefit both to the teachings and to real people.

After that he made his way back to Tibet, where he discovered that there were major civil disturbances occurring in the regions of both Uw and Tsang. Some of the people were actually undergoing serious suffering, while others were reveling in the act of creating future suffering for themselves. When he looked upon all these things he was overcome by a deep sadness, and composed the following *Song of a Breaking Heart*.

Parting Words on the Steps

This short piece summarizes some important steps of the path. It was composed around the Panchen Rinpoche's sixti-

eth year, and is from pp. 546-547 of Master Tsechok Ling's Brief Biography.

In those days he wrote many songs of his spiritual life, including this one.

The History of Pain

We continue with rare examples of His Holiness the First Panchen Lama's poetry, located in papers at the Tantric College of Trashi Hlunpo Monastery by his biographer, Yongdzin Yeshe Gyeltsen (1713-1793). The following selection is found at pp. 559-560 of the Brief Biography, *and records His Holiness' final words—still begging us to love all beings.*

There came a time when almost all the personal disciples who had followed him in this life had already passed on themselves. As a portent of his decision to move to a different realm, his holy body transformed completely: he shrank to the size of a child of only eight years, and his complexion became smooth as a baby's. He seemed to be made of light itself.

He remained unshakeable in the deepest state of mind. Between his meditation sessions, he would suddenly blurt out all kinds of things, driven by the power of his love. Over and over he would say things (like this poem)—words about how we should be inspired by the infinite power of the Wish for enlightenment, never feeling discouraged as we work for the good of every living being, until the day that the universe itself draws to an end.

All the people of faith then—led by the monks of Trashi Hlunpo—approached him, beseeching him with the words, "Please keep your lotus feet planted in this world. We beg you to grant us a verse that we can use as a prayer for your long life."

In an instant then he blurted out the following gift
to them:

The second Buddha, Lobsang Drakpa,
Has raised the flag of victory—
The open and secret teachings.
May its burning light
Ban the darkness
Within infinite disciples,
And open lotus blooms
Of a thousand petals
In pleasure gardens
Of help and happiness.

Then he gave a little chuckle and said, "Not to worry.
Don't worry about some senile hundred-year-old. Instead
may our Precious Lama Tsongkapa's lotus feet remain
strong in this world, for the glory of the teachings." He
refused thus to agree to stay among us.

In the year called Goodness then—that is, in the
male water tiger year 1662—on the 13th day of the
month of Fragrance, the time for him to withdraw his
holy form came upon us. He folded his legs in the
lotus posture, passed into meditation, and trans-
formed himself into the body of reality: to clear light
itself.

Throw Off the Iron Fetters

*In this selection His Holiness the First Panchen Lama reacts
to the threat of impending death with advice to his monks
that they should master self-control—not only in the sense of
keeping ones commitments, but by refraining from the Eight
Worldly Dharmas: happy when we get something, unhappy
when we don't; happy when we get some fame, unhappy when we
don't; happy when others say nice things to us, unhappy when*

they don't; happy when we feel good, unhappy when we don't.

In the year of Youth then—which would be the female wood pig year [1635]—there were terrible signs of impending doom: great inner and outer portents of upheaval. Many of the Lord's major disciples, headed by the lamas of Trashi Hlunpo, came to him, begging him, saying that a ceremony for his long life must be conducted, imploring him to allow that rituals be held to prevent any obstacles to his health.

The Lord though refused to have any such ceremonies undertaken. He persisted in following in the footsteps of the great adepts of the past: he simply continued on in tasks like smashing and flattening the Eight Worldly Thoughts in his own mind; and working to turn everything that happened—good or bad—into a path to something higher. At this point he also came out with these words on smashing those same eight thoughts.

Song of the Realized Being

More rare poetry from His Holiness the First Panchen Lama, again from the Brief Biography *of Yongdzin Yeshe Gyeltsen. His Holiness is about fifty when he has this sudden insight into the pain of his life, something that relates to every step of the path.*

He received then an invitation to Drepung, and he went. There he imparted the entire empowerment of the *String of Diamonds,* sitting within a huge globe of light like the sun itself, surrounded by high beings such as His Holiness Yunten Gyatso [the Fourth Dalai Lama], Simkang Gong Trulku, and other incarnate Lamas of both Sera and Drepung.

During these days he was touring a great deal, far and wide, providing a fertile garden in which disciples of faith could plant the seeds of their good karma. He saw with his own holy eyes how things were in a state of constant flux: how none of the places, or the events, or the people, or anything at all could stay without changing for even a moment.

This triggered in him an understanding, something that came upon him without the slightest conscious effort. He saw how every single supposed good thing in the cycle of pain was actually like a dinner party in a dream, or the play of some illusion. He saw how the very way of all things that come into being is like a dance of lightning, or the random gathering and dissolution of clouds in the sky. He saw how the life of beings here in the age of degeneration was brief as a bubble, or morning dew on the tip of a blade of grass.

Above all, he saw that—from the moment he had entered the womb—his life had lain in the jaws of the Lord of Death. He saw that—since there were so many things around him all the time that could kill him—then there was absolutely no guarantee that he would survive any particular day. In fact, it became a source of wonder to him that death hadn't struck him down already.

And so it occurred to him that right now, in just this instant, he could be close to taking the final journey. Fierce thoughts of renunciation sprang up in his heart, and he penned the following *Song of the Realized Being* to express how he felt.

Song of a Burning Heart

We see the depths to which His Holiness the First Panchen Lama's sadness over the state of the world could fall.

At the urging then of a great mass of faithful people, he traveled to the lands of Dringtsam and Chenlung. Everywhere he went, he planted the seeds of freedom within his disciples. He then continued on to Jangpuk, in Sar, where he was able to meet the image of Lord Atisha. He made offerings to the image, and prayers as well—and then suddenly he was overcome by an intense feeling of sadness about life, and composed the *Song of a Burning Heart*.

Get Yourself to Some Wild Desert Place

His Holiness the First Panchen Lama is not much more than 50 years old when he writes this song to the joys of meditation, dreaming of a place that sounds a lot like Diamond Mountain. Still from the Brief Biography *of Yongdzin Yeshe Gyeltsen.*

He composed this song as a heart-prayer that he would be able to take himself to some isolated place, and devote his entire attention to his practice.

The Dance of the Daughter

His Holiness the First Panchen Lama is probably in his mid-fifties when he composes this wondrous song to emptiness. Again taken from Yongdzin Yeshe Gyeltsen's Brief Biography.

Rainbow Arching over the Path to Deathlessness

His Holiness the First Panchen Lama is still in his thirties when he writes the following poem to describe an experience of emptiness. The selection is, again, from the Brief Biography *of Yongdzin Yeshe Gyeltsen.*

He traveled once more to Trashi Hlunpo; as soon as the ceremonies for the end of the monks' summer retreat there were completed, he went into deep retreat.

It occurred to him suddenly that—even though being in retreat was a virtuous thing to do—in his case it was all just a big mistake, hour after hour spent totally wrapped up in some kind of distracted daze. He decided that everything he was doing with his life was all meaningless, nothing more than a big façade, nothing what it appeared to be. And that triggered within him a naked, raw perception of deceptive reality. This then immediately caused an actual image of the emptiness of true reality to come up powerfully within his mind—and he uttered these lines.

The Union of the Two

His Holiness is again still in his thirties when he pens another poem to emptiness.

Naked, Dressed in the Robe of Emptiness

A poem from His Holiness the First Panchen Lama on how empty things still work, to stop the pain of the world.

In those days he threw himself into the practice of that most profound of all things: the one thing that the Buddha really had in mind with everything he ever taught. And the following thought came up within his holy mind:

> Suppose I were able to devote my heart entirely to that pair: to the emptiness yogas of balanced meditation and subsequent wisdom. And suppose I were able to maintain these yogas over some period of time. I don't see how it would be any difficult thing then to perceive emptiness directly.

He was able thus to attain an extraordinary insight into the way of profound dependent origination—a way which has as its distinctive feature the unique position of the Consequence Group of the Middle Way: the belief that an understanding of what appears to us prevents the extreme of thinking that things exist the way they seem; while an understanding of emptiness prevents the opposite extreme, of thinking that nothing exists at all. He then wrote this song of spiritual experience.

By the goodness of this deed may the work become a victory banner (*gyeltsen*) which flies above the precious teachings, so that they never disappear from our world.

Mangalam!
Joyful Fortune for All!

By the goodness of this task I've done
May I and every living being
Come to the final end of the practice
For people of three different scopes.

Om swasti!
Om! Goodness be to all.

The teachings of the Victorious Ones
Are a great tree where living beings assemble,
A source of help and happiness.
It spreads its mighty branches and then
Every living creature comes
To pluck that finest fruit
Of the highest form of freedom.
May the tree be fed by the gentle waters
Of an inexhaustible stream of the gift
Of the Dharma, evermore increasing
Here within the walls of the abbey
Where joyful fortune appears of its own.[24]

Sarva Dzagatam:
For the sake of every living being.

This collection of most profound insight is provided here to get the essence of life—to successfully manifest the practice of ultimate love and wisdom, uniting the two. Any errors are the responsibility of the editor, who compiled this holy work in appreciation of The Teacher's kindness. These glorious verses were translated by Arya Sumati Dharmadhara, Geshe Michael Roach, with Christie McNally. They were presented at Diamond Mountain in 2004, alongside De Lam, The Path to Bliss, *as part of a tantric teacher training program.*

Notes

1 The Tibetan word *drak* here appears to be a play on the ordination name of Je Tsongkapa: Lobsang Drakpa.

2 The way that the Tibetan reads here, "his" could refer either to Je Tsongkapa or to His Holiness.

3 Celebrating the Dharma, or goodness, is perhaps the greatest good we can accomplish.

4 The sign of a thousand-spoked Dharma wheel on the palms of the hands and soles of the feet; extra webbing connecting the fingers and toes; and a gilded look to the fingernails and toenails are some of the signs on the body of an enlightened being.

5 The "Man of the Sugarcane" is an epithet of Lord Buddha, as he belonged to a race of people called "The People of the Sugarcane."

6 Shuddhodana was the father of Lord Buddha.

7 The "five kings" seem to be His Holiness' once-powerful organs of sense. "The Peak" is a name for the final level of the formless realm, which is thus the highest possible level we can reach within the cycle of pain.

8 The "three" here are the three bodies of a Buddha, or three forms of kindness that a Lama shows their disciple.

9 The "Second Buddha" here refers to Je Tsongkapa.

10 The five degenerations are a shortening of the average life span; an increase in the length and force of mental afflictions in people's minds; a degeneration in the personalities of people, becoming more and more difficult to turn to a spiritual life; the coming of an era of violence; and a worsening of people's wordview.

11 Shuddhodana was the father of Lord Buddha.

12 "Mati Bhadra" is the Sanskrit equivalent for the Tibetan "Lobsang," which is the first part of Je Tsongkapa's ordination name.

13 The "Second Buddha" in this case refers to Je Tsongkapa.

14 "Lighter of Lamps" is the literal meaning of the other Sanskrit name by which Lord Atisha was known: Dipamkara.

15 The Tibetans translated the names of almost all the teachers from India, but Lord Atisha was an exception. His Holiness the First Panchen Lama was probably one of the very few to realize that the literal meaning of the Sanskrit name Atisha is "Perfect One."

16 Dromtun Je ("Lord Drom") had the spiritual name of Gyalway Jungne, or "Source of the Victorious Buddhas."

17 The Brahmin Tsanakya followed a high ritual for the Lord of Death and used it to harm many people, which led him to a birth in the realms of hell.

18 The "three" mentioned here could have many meanings. One is that our Lama has granted us the three different types of kindness. In the system of the open teachings, they grant us personal advice; oral transmissions; and formal instruction. In the system of the secret teachings, they grant us empowerments; explanations of the secret books; and private instruction on these subjects.

19 The five mental-affliction poisons are listed as ignorant liking of things; ignorant disliking of things; dark ignorance itself; pride; and jealousy.

20 The "longbow of the Lord of Power" is a poeticism for the rainbow.

21 The twelve-count practice here refers to the deeds of deep practitioners who give up the world and are thus known by twelve different names: people who live in garbage dumps; those who wear the three robes; those who dress in rags; those of a single seat; those who go begging for their food; those who take no food later in the day; those who stay in hermitages; those who sleep at the foot of a tree; those who have no roof over their heads; those who live in the burial ground; those who live in filth; and those who lie down to sleep wherever they happen to be.

22 The reference to white and red fingernails seems to mean "the hands of men and women (who painted their fingernails)".

23 The "five great terrors" are listed differently in different places. In the famous Steps of the Teaching (*Tenrim Chenmo*) by Geshe Drolungpa, they are said to be the terror of death among the pleasure beings; the terror of desire among humans; the terror of attack among the hellbeings; the terror of eating and being eaten among the animals; and the terror of unbearable hunger and thirst among the craving spirits.

24 The expression "joyful fortune that appears of its own" includes all the words that make up the name of Trashi Hlunpo Monastery, seat of His Holiness the Panchen Lama.